Ike's Travels

Ike Gramlich

Published by:

Eagle Ghost Writers
www.eagleghostwriters.com

Printed in the United States of America

Dedication

To put my thoughts into perspective, I must recall what took me on this journey of writing.

Never having written other than some essays in high school, some technical reports at university, and starting a Family Farming History but never finishing it, the task to start writing has been a steep learning curve.

But this story is an expansion of the factual story, 'A Backpack and A Dream', told to commemorate my brother's journey, but in a different way.

I am the traveller, retracing a portion of my brother's journey, and I am experiencing what my imagination brings to paper.

So I dedicate this story to my brother Les, who is my inspiration. I have a very spiritual friend who advises me to connect with my brother Les. He is no longer with us, but she advises that my subconscious is tuned into my brother on a level that most of us think is hogwash.

I also dedicate this story to the readers out there who travel. The world was considerably different from 1965 to 1970, when my brother travelled all the continents, sixty plus countries with little money to start and had a backpack and a dream.

So to all readers, travel with care, plan well, and think of my story as very plausible. In 2027, I intend to actually complete this journey I have told and then write a factual story of that trip.

Acknowledgment

I would like to thank my parents for raising me, helping develop the skills, education and personality I have today. The farm upbringing on a mixed farm and eleven siblings existed and flourished with their dedication, spirit, guidance and love. We worked very hard, we were treated fairly, and we were fed well. We were expected to respect our siblings, parents, uncles, aunts, other adults and our friends.

I would also like to acknowledge my eleven siblings for their parts in developing my character, my imagination and my skills. From them, I learned cooperation and respect. We worked hard, played hard and often fought hard.

My two wives taught me patience, communication skills and a little about love.

My children taught me tolerance, patience and lots about love. This book is for them to reach out with their imaginations and try things that may seem unattainable.

To my readers who took a chance to read an amateur's work, laugh at me and hopefully with me. I hope you have the interest to find or request Ike's Travels books 2,3, 4 and on.

To my editors and publishers, thank you for the assistance and patience working with me and completing our tasks.

About the Author

Ike Gramlich was born September 4, 1950, number 9 of 12 children on a central Alberta mixed farm.

Ike completed High School and then attended Northern Alberta Institute of Technology, graduating in Civil Engineering.

His career included working in municipal infrastructure and industrial oil, gas and power supply projects. Ike also worked extensively across the Arctic in many isolated communities, infrastructure projects and mine and early warning radar sites cleanup projects.

As a young man, Ike travelled 8 months backpacking around Europe, has been on many trips to the Caribbean and an Asian trip with his son.

Ike always dreamed of following his older brother's journey around the world. To accomplish this, Ike has written a fiction story of travelling from Canada to New Zealand, Australia, the Philippines, Singapore, Malaysia, Thailand, Pakistan, India, Nepal, India and Sweden.

In 2027, his plan is to travel the first leg of his brother's journey, with an itinerary already set from this first novel. There will be a follow-up novel of his first-hand experience of this trip.

As part of completing a legacy to his brother, Ike plans on 2-3 more fiction novels about travels through the Middle East, Europe, Africa, South America, and Central America. Ike plans to travel these next novel routes with his first-hand experience portrayed in future stories.

Table of Contents

Chapter 1
Border Crossing

On my trip from New Delhi to the Pakistan border, the train was jam-packed with mostly people, but in the last portion, chickens, dogs, and a few small pigs were mixed in. On the train, an Indian or Pakistani man, I was not sure which, was talking to me. I noticed he had been talking to a white female, but she had pointed at me, so he came to talk to me.

He spoke enough English that we were talking, and he was interested in where I had come from, whether I knew anyone in India, and where I was going. In a country like India, there are many scam artists, and they are after your money, so I stopped talking to this man.

I was quite relieved to depart the train at the rail station at Dhawam Colony, which made it necessary to take a bus to Karian and then the JDC Sadqi Indo-Pak border crossing. It is very isolated and mountainous in this border crossing location.

The day seemed quite normal; the border crossing was a little out of the way, but the bus ride was not long. The man who had been talking to me on the train was tagging along with me.

Arriving at the border was typical of isolated borders such as these. It was manned by few, and the border guards were similar to others in this part of the world where the staff manning these crossings are generally not as professional, are poorly trained and do not have much money or morals.

Security is minimal, and one is always concerned for one's personal safety. I was wondering if I would have to bribe a guard. The people from this part of the world, whether Pakistani or Indian, had no issue with crossing; they were more or less waved through. A white person such as me is a different story. We are a target for the guards to pursue and possibly get some much-needed cash in their pockets to help feed their families.

The man from the train was there and started talking to the Indian guards. I noticed the man had passed a bribe to the guard, and I was wondering what was going on. As my turn came, I approached the guard; I was not hassled, my bag was not checked, and I was stamped out of India.

After walking across to the Pakistani side, I sensed a different atmosphere. Today was not unusual, in that my bag had to be emptied with a search for drugs or anything of value that they would suggest I could not bring across. I have reduced my belongings to prevent any such issue with goods like carvings, souvenirs, or anything that can catch the guard's eye—and especially no drugs.

The one guard took my passport and went into their little hut and was conversing on the phone. This was not a good sign, as they are either going to detain you or arrange some other fate for you with whoever they were contacting. I was wondering where the man from the train was, but I could not locate him.

The guard came out of the hut, and at this time, all hell broke loose. Many armed and hooded men came out of the nearby bush, and from behind the hut, the guard that had taken my passport put his weapon on the ground. The other guard shouldered his weapon to resist the armed gang and was immediately shot by multiple gang members using their automatic weapons. I hit the ground as I did not want to be shot.

Many of the locals that had crossed the border were running in all directions for cover and were not any threat to this armed gang. I stayed on the ground, covering my head with my pack. After one guard was shot, the other guard picked up the shot guard's weapon and his own—it became apparent that he was a gang member. He immediately started conversing with the gang members like he was their leader and I was the center of the discussion. There was nothing I could do, or my life would have been in danger.

Two pickup trucks came from different directions, and I was unceremoniously thrown into the back of one pickup, and all the gang members loaded up on the trucks. The trucks were leaving the area in a hurry, and we traveled on a dirt path away from the hut and road into the bush. The drivers knew this trail, and we traveled for more than an hour over extremely difficult terrain with the trucks using four-wheeled drive most of the time.

It became obvious to me that I was their target to be abducted in this manner. I knew that I had no choice but to remain subdued and try to relax, but I was scared to death. I had only read about such abductions, and usually, the target's life is in mortal danger. I noticed one of the gang members was trying to conceal his face with a hoodie, but I was quite sure it was the man from the train.

We arrived at a camp of ragtag huts and tents. There were approximately ten of the gang members all combined, and I was taken to a tent that covered a cave of sorts. There was a steel door; they opened and shoved me inside. The light was very poor, but a female voice immediately spoke to me; she was not far from me. She came towards me and was looking at me.

Before they had closed and locked the door, I had a good look at this other prisoner; she looked as scared as I felt and was about my height and from my quick look, she was beautiful. She started speaking to me in a shaky voice, but it was not English; she was speaking India's main language, Hindhi, which I knew very little.

I took her hand and put it on my chest and said my name, Ike. She spoke good English and asked me what I was doing here, and I told her how I was abducted from the border. Then she hugged me and was crying and shaking, saying she was so glad to have me to speak to and would not let me go.

I was also quite relieved of not being alone in this predicament and asked who she was. Her name was Richa Chadha; she said she was kidnapped in Mumbai, India. That is all we had time for as the door was opened, and we were taken out to the trucks, and it was obvious that the gang was moving.

We traveled about another hour till darkness was starting to settle in; the gang stopped and were discussing their plans. I had been placed in one truck and Richa in the other, so I had no chance to talk to her.

The gang leader sat us down together, and he spoke to her in Hindi, and I think he was questioning her about me. There was a lot of pointing at me, and I think Richa differed with him; at one point, he grabbed her by her blouse front and jerked her to her feet, shouting at her.

When he did this, he instructed another gang member who came to my side, and he placed a pistol to my head. I almost shit my pants as I thought this was it, and I was being shot. Richa screamed and was again talking to the leader. The gun was taken away from my head, and Richa dropped to the ground and was crying.

The guy who had a gun to my head grabbed me and shoved me to the ground beside Richa. When she had stopped crying, the leader was telling her to talk to me. She explained that they wanted to use me as part of their plan to get money from her mother in exchange for her life. I understood their intent but was not sure how all this would take place; I had no choice but to wait.

There was much discussion with gang members, especially with the man from the train and their leader. The man from the train approached me and explained to me that I was to be used as a courier for receiving money from Richa's mother and was to bring it back to Pakistan. He would accompany me back to New Delhi, and when I was in contact with Richa's mother, he would at all times be watching me, and if I did not do as they suggested, he would call the gang in Pakistan to harm Richa.

Here I was, after traveling for two month's with a beautiful Swedish woman, Ina. We parted in Katmandu, and she and her parents were returning to Sweden. After our troubles in Thailand that turned out ok, I was off on this trip across the Middle East, retracing my brother's route. There were many warnings about my safety, to which I assured them that I would be fine.

Now, here I was a few days after leaving them, kidnapped and being forced into a scheme to force a young woman's mother to pay a ransom. I was extremely terrified and worried. I also was extremely angry at being in a difficult situation again with scumbag terrorists.

What was really amazing to me was that the name Chadha was ringing a bell in my memory. About fifteen years ago, I was visiting my nephew in Mumbai, India, where he worked. We were at a party one evening, and I was introduced to this movie star whose last name was Chadha. Could this other captive be her daughter?

Chapter 2
"Arrival New Zealand"

A man has many aspirations, wishes, and dreams, and life goes on at a speed that many of us do not realize till we age. I am no different, and as my busy life progressed through a career, a family, and then a divorce, a second family, and another divorce, some of my aspirations and dreams were fulfilled. I have traveled some in my life, and I often found it was a trill, and it expanded one's view of many things. I did not like the getting to a destination part of travel; it often involved a specific time frame, which often is compromised.

My brother traveled for four years and one hundred and seventy days, and the related experiences and stories were incredible. There was no specific time frame for his journey. His main task was working his way around the world, which restricted his choice of travel modes. I had been thinking of his journey, and maybe I could retrace portions of his route, albeit with more choices of traveling modes, as I would have more funds. I have to consider my age, which restricts the amount of walking and packing a backpack, such as my brother did.

I reviewed my brother's route, which started in Edmonton, Alberta, Canada. My parents gave him a ride to Vancouver, and he hitchhiked from Vancouver to Los Angeles. He knew that finding a job on a ship bound for New Zealand would be more successful at a busy port like Los Angeles.

Since I cannot enter the USA, long story, I chose Vancouver for my attempts to find a ship bound for New Zealand. I have friends in Vancouver I looked up to stay with while I searched for a job on a ship. I thought it was better to be in Vancouver, and if a job was available, it maybe would give only a moment's notice for departure.

I also researched booking passenger passage on a ship or airline flights as alternative options. I wanted to experience as much as my brother's journey in the manner he did it. I travelled by air to Vancouver and stayed at my friend's home.

I searched the docks, loading terminals, and shipping offices, and it was a difficult quest to find a job on a ship. There were many hurdles, and it seemed I was doomed to buy passage on a ship or airline. As I was cooking supper with my friend, my cell phone buzzed, and I was in for a surprise. A shipping company was offering a cook helper job on a container ship from Vancouver to New Zealand. I was excited but also apprehensive; the ship departed in two days.

When I was downsizing at my home in Alberta, I had chosen a backpack that I had, and it was good quality and light, so this was my choice for traveling with. I sorted through all required clothing, toiletries, some over-the-counter drugs for digestion and painkillers, camera equipment, cell phone, and charger and packed carefully. I would travel as lightly as possible and purchase what I needed as required.

Money in today's world is not a problem compared to when my brother went from 1966 to 1970; he had cash or traveler's cheques. Even the traveler's cheques were a problem with the banks in some countries, as they were concerned about the time required to get their money from the Canadian bank, which was all by mail. I am taking $3000 US cash and two credit cards, and I would utilize my credit cards as much as possible. My fanny pack will always be on my person with money and passport.

I boarded the ship on **Monday, January 10, 2026**. My cabin/birth was small but sufficient, and I could lock my door. Washroom facilities were shared with other crew members, and we had a cafeteria-style eating area.

I was introduced to my chef/cook, my boss. He spoke good English, and he toured me through the kitchen and storage areas. He explained what my work duties were, the schedule for meals, and what he expected from me. He suggested he ran a tight ship and would not tolerate a slacker as he keeps his domain sparkling clean. His name was Jari, he was from Finland, and he had been the cook on this ship for three years.

The crew consisted of the Captain (chief mate), first and second mates, Chief Engineer and Second Engineer, a motorman, Chief Steward, one chief cook and assistant, one communications technician, and four deckhands.

The ship was considered a Panamax size, the name coming from the ship's size, which could fit through the Panama Canal. She could carry a maximum of 80,000 DWT tons. She was a container ship. I had never sailed on any ship, so I was interested to find out more details about this ship. Her name was 'Sabrina,' owned by a Chinese company and registered in Panama. She was 290 m long and 32 m wide with a draft of 12 meters with a twin bottom. I was told by the engineer that she recently had repairs completed on the engine, drive mechanism, and propellers.

The ship was underway at the scheduled departure time and date, **leaving Vancouver on Jan 11, 2026**. After clearing the San Juan Islands and the Salish Sea, we were steaming a straight line for Hawaii, and I recalled my brother expressing feelings of great loneliness on the wide open sea. It does not hit you till day after day; all you see is the ocean, hear the same wind noise, hear the same ship's engines throbbing, and the ship's hulls groan.

I settled into my job as the chef was great to work with. He allowed me to cook some things and was surprised at what I called my 'goulash.' He knew this name from his Finnish/Russian heritage but had never cooked it much. The crew had positive comments on Jari's new dish, and he just smiled and pointed at me.

The work was quite hard for a seventy-six-year-old; Jari told me in a positive way that I worked hard for an old man. Since I was experienced at cooking for family and friends groups of up to twenty, I recognized the quantities required and helped Jari with these plans. We got along great, but I was really tired after the first three to four days, and it was difficult.

We arrived in Hawaii in 7 days; the weather had been mostly favorable and storm-free. My thoughts were that the ocean was quite rough, but little did I know I had never experienced a larger storm. The ship rolled with the mild to medium seas, and you got used to the shift in your step as required; I guess you could say you 'rolled with the ship.' Hawaii was primarily a refueling stop, and we took on a few fresh food supplies.

Back underway from Hawaii to Auckland, New Zealand, the trip usually takes between fifteen to twenty days if all weather conditions are favorable. We mostly followed a straight line, but there was a diversion to pass around a storm, which cost us about 2 days of sailing time.

This storm scared me considerably, but Jari and the crew laughed at me, the greenhorn. I did not get seasick, but I felt out of sorts with the changing rhythm of the ship's normal rolling motion to a much quicker chopping roll, and the noises from the ship were much louder.

We arrived in Auckland, New Zealand, **Feb 8, 2026**. I had many discussions with Jari during our time working together; he was very interested to hear about my brother's four-and-a-half-year journey. As we neared Auckland, he asked me at different times if I was jumping ship in New Zealand, and I always told him, of course, otherwise, how could I retrace my brother's route?

We had worked together really well, and he was not enthused about training a new helper. I had spoken to the Captain about this also. There were many discussions about my brother's trip with crew members, and the Captain was not concerned that I was leaving his ship to pursue my brother's route.

After docking at Mechanics Bay, the container handling facility, I said my farewells to the ship's crew; Jari had packed me enough food for days.

I researched about the Haka House youth hostel, which is in downtown Auckland, very near the container ship handling facility. Even an old man can use a youth hostel. I grabbed a cab to get there and arrived at the Haka House near noon.

"Arrival New Zealand"

Since I have not traveled extensively using youth hostels, I was satisfied with my first choice. It was cheap at $69/night for a private room. I wanted to slowly learn to use hostels that are cheaper, so my first experience at Haku was upper scale; as hostels go, I would soon learn. I could lock my room, I had my own bathroom, the kitchen facilities were great, and the travel desk had lots of info and a bulletin board for travelers to share information or request travel companions.

I shared some of my food with a couple from the south island, and they suggested I leave my name on the board that I wish to share vehicle expenses with someone traveling the north and south islands.

I had a list of things to see and do in Auckland, so I relaxed and planned my first day. Auckland is a very popular destination for vacationers and sailors, which tends to make the cost of everything higher.

For my first night out, I was told to stay away from K-road as it has a certain crowd it attracts, consisting of hippies, political activists, feminists, LGBTQI types, drag queens, and kings, so not my crowd. I was told Ponsonby Street and The Viaduct Waterfront would suit me better. I looked up Danny Doolan's and spent a few hours there, enjoying the Irish music and atmosphere.

My night was quiet, the shower water was hot, and the bed was comfortable. The next day, I checked out the bulletin board, and there was a note to contact Missy. She and a friend are driving around both islands and would like to meet.

They were at the kitchen facility at 10, and I found them easily, as they were the only two females by themselves. I introduced myself, and we started talking about the normal stuff, where we were from, and where we hoped to go. I think they were disappointed with my age but, at the same time, likely felt safe with me.

They were from England, had seen the sights in Auckland, and had a list of things on both the north and south islands they wished to visit. They had rented a Kia SUV and planned about a 2-week trip. I suggested I was certainly interested and had a list of things I wanted to see also.

I brought out the food that Jari had packed for me and shared it with them. They were impressed that I had worked on a ship to get here, and I told them about my brother's journey around the world and was attempting to follow part of his route.

After chatting, they wanted to think about traveling with me and would meet later to go out for the evening. I was quite interested in them; I thought they were likely about 35 years old and were looking for a safe traveler to help with expenses. Missy was a little chubby but not excessive, and Cherri was gorgeous and looked really fit.

We met at 7 pm, and they took me to a pub they knew. They liked beer, and we were getting along really well. I had the feeling they enjoyed my company and conversation. I told them about my experience in Europe when I was eighteen and hooked up with two teachers from Boston in Germany and I travelled with them in a VW van for three month's to southern Europe and back to England.

They were very curious about my brother's trip. I showed them a map of his route; they were fascinated. I explained that after touring New Zealand, I would look up Ted and Tessie Cross in Sydney, look for a good used VW van or something similar, and travel to Melbourne, Adelaide, Alice Springs, and Darwin.

I explained that once in Darwin, I would sell the van and then plan the next leg going north through Indonesia, Malaysia, Thailand, Burma, Bangladesh, and India. After returning to Haka House, we agreed to meet in the morning, and they would decide whether to travel with me or not.

I slept well and was hopeful Missy and Cherri would decide to travel with me. At the hostel kitchen in the morning, Missy and Cherri came to my table, and both agreed to travel with me. we discussed sharing vehicle, food, shared rooms costs, or separate

16

rooms if desired. We would meet in about two hours and start our journey.

The rented Kia SUV had plenty of space; the girls were traveling quite light, similar to me, so everything fit in the back cargo area without difficulty. We did not have sleeping bags, as we planned on staying in hostels or cheap hotels. I suggested we purchase a large cooler and always have fruit, water, and snacks with us.

We started going north from Auckland to Marsden Point on day one, Feb 11. 2026. Missy was a great driver; I preferred to have these young girls do all the driving. We found a nice bed and breakfast near the beach and settled in, then went to the beach.

That evening, there was plenty of activity along the beach bars, and we sampled the beers and food. Back at our bed and breakfast, we settled in for the night. I drew the short straw and had the fold-out couch.

I found the girls were understandably shy about their nakedness, so I respected their privacy. Chrissie commented that I had a good body for an old guy when I came out of the shower with a towel wrapped around me. I explained that I sleep naked, and they both giggled about that.

On day two, the scenery was beautiful all the way north to the ninety-mile beach. We were thrilled to be zipping along the sand and found a group of surfers and stopped to have lunch and some beers with them.

They had a makeshift camp set up and invited us to stay the night with them. We had not come prepared for sleeping out, so we declined. Once on our way back south, Missy said she was glad the old man was with them as the surfers were a rough and tumble bunch and made them a little nervous.

Heading back south, we went to the east coast to see the Harura Falls and, at Paihia, found the Aloha Seaview Resort Motel for $69. The girls were ok with one room; they got the double bed, and I had the single cot.

We had supper from our cooler supplies with the little kitchenette. I cooked a goulash throw-together of spicy noodle soup with onions, carrots, garlic, cabbage, and smoked sausage. The girls had seconds and declared that I am the official cook if I so choose.

Being in one room, I warned the girls that my goulash sometimes creates some unexpected venting of maybe colorful odors during my sleep, so beware. Missy said, 'So you fart does you,' which caused lots of laughing. The night passed peacefully, odor-free, and neither girl snuck into my cot.

On day three, we were traveling back along Highway 1, going right through Auckland, as I discovered the girls prefer smaller places to big cities like Auckland, which is my choice also.

South of Auckland, we arrived in Hamilton and went west to a bed and breakfast, the Waitomo Orchard B&B for $79, near the glowworm caves. We settled in and went to our scheduled guided tour of the Glowworm caves.

Back at the B&B, we enjoyed the peace and quiet and a nice hot tub to soak in with nice cold beers to boot. Our conversations involved many questions about each of our families, our jobs, and our countries. I was designated on the fold-out couch.

On day four, Feb 14, 2026, Valentine's Day, after a scrumptious breakfast with Kiwi fruit salad, we continued west to Raglan to watch surfers, as this is the best surfer destination. Then we traveled to Huka Falls and Lake Taupo and then continued on to Mt Ngauruhoeto to see the active volcano.

The next stop was near Mt Ruapehu ski resort, where my brother had worked bartending. We made Taihape that night at the Rusty Nail Backpackers Lodge. In Taihape, I was fortunate to find a shop with Valentine's boxes of chocolates that I offered the girls that night with cold beers.

"Arrival New Zealand"

On day five, we arrived at Wellington and found the Nomads Capital Hostel for $36/night, settled in, and went touring the sights around the city. We found a sports complex with a steam room and hot tub and spent a few hours there.

We researched the ferry for the next day from Wellington to Picton on the South Island, which sailed the next morning for $185 for the car with passengers. Our advice was to go to Cuba Street for supper and nightlife. After our night out of drinking, we had hangovers the next morning, and with the fantastic weather, we decided to stay a second night in Wellington.

On day seven, we boarded the ferry from **Wellington to Picton at 8 am, Feb 17**, for a 5 hr ride through fantastic scenery and met a bunch of backpackers and travelers.

I had struck up a conversation with a beautiful girl from Sweden, Ina. She had been hitchhiking and not having good luck with rides. After more discussion with Missy and Cherri, Ina was very curious about how an old guy was traveling with Missy and Cherri.

After explaining our meeting and travel plans, Ina asked if we had room for one more; the girls asked me if we could squeeze her in, how could I refuse??? Ina was so energetic and quite pretty, so she was surely to liven up our times.

My thoughts centered on how to choose sleeping accommodations with three girls if we chose to have one room with sufficient beds. The SUV became more crowded, but we all were traveling light with one backpack each and a large cooler; it all fit in.

Missy had researched the Tombstone Backpackers Lodge. It had a dormitory-type room with single beds for up to eight, and we arrived at about 2 pm and unpacked. Ina was curious how we chose our rooms with two females and one male. Missy and Cherri suggested the old guy was a gentleman, and we had shared six nights with various accommodations.

In Picton, yachting is very popular, so it was a very cosmopolitan crowd and atmosphere. We went shopping for travel food and a place to eat and have some beers. The girls were chatting steadily with Ina about where she had traveled and where she was going.

I had determined that all the girls were possibly on an extensive holiday, but they did not have unlimited funds, which is why we were sharing our rental SUV and picking rooms that had multiple beds and a shared bathroom.

I was quiet for the most part and answered questions as required. We all talked a lot about our families with questions both ways. We had not discussed any travel plans besides the south island and eventually being back on the north island to Auckland, where the rental had to be returned.

We found a waterfront pub and were having beers. I asked the girls how long they were planning on traveling and where their destinations were. Ina had flown from Sweden to New Zealand with a stop in Bangkok, Thailand, for three days and did not like the big city. She had arrived in Auckland one week ago and traveled to Wellington hitchhiking, but suggested rides were not frequent, and she was concerned about her safety. She was happy to travel with us as we had a good vehicle and there was safety in numbers, especially one male who could have been their father. Her future plans were to cross to Australia with no specific destinations. She had about two to three month's of duration in her plans, depending on how long her funds lasted. She liked the sharing of travel costs that Missy, Cherri, and I were doing.

Missy and Cherri had flown from London, England, to a three-day stop in Riyadh, Saudi Arabia, and were impressed with the sites, but everything there was expensive, and they did not really like the culture; they could not drink. They had enjoyed their stay in New Zealand much more than in Saudi Arabia, and travel with me helped costs, and they suggested that they have enjoyed my company. They also had plans to cross to Australia and did not have specific destinations except the south coastline. They had about one-month duration left on their plan with no specific destinations, but funds limited their plans also. They liked sharing costs with me and suggested I was a good cook and planned travel food very well like I had done it forever. They had never traveled much, especially this way.

Missy asked me to describe to Ina my brother's journey around the world. I had explained some of it to Missy and Cherri, so I told them about his journey again and showed them the little Falcon map I had on my phone and photos of his route. They were all very impressed, and Ina asked what my travel plans were. I explained the story I had written about Les's journey, and I was starting on my ultimate plans to retrace his journey. This portion may take me to India or Nepal and home from there.

Ina commented that I am a crazy old man and it was such a different world from when my brother did it, so how was I ever to accomplish this? I totally agreed with her and explained this portion of the retracing would take me through the Aussie outback with a good vehicle I was going to buy in Sydney. I would sell it in Darwin and carry on through the Indonesian islands and Malaysia, then detour from his route to the Philippines.

I explained that my former renter and long-time friends Barry and Liberty had built a house there, and I would stay there for a while. Then, continue through Malaysia, Thailand, Burma,

Bangladesh, and India. In New Delhi, I planned a trip to Nepal and find a yoga and meditation retreat for one month.

The questions never stopped about how I was to accomplish this and whether I was rich. No, I was not rich, but I had some retirement funds and was attempting to enjoy life to its fullest and then possibly write a book about my trip. I showed them my story of Les's four-year, one hundred and seventy-day journey.

I explained that I was not considering traveling to the Middle East as it was too unpredictable. Europe, I saw as a kid and would do more with a motorcycle if my health was ok. My plan was to go down Africa but with better modes of transportation than Les had for options. But now, it is so different and unsafe. South America is also difficult and unsafe.

Missy and Cherri wanted to go with me on this first leg of my journey but had limited time and funds. They had to fly back from Australia; they complained that they would have to use credit cards. Ina, however, had got up at one point when I came back from the bathroom, hugged me, and said, 'I am your companion to India if you would have me.'

This whole discussion with many beers was such a pleasure; here I was, an old man chatting with three lovely, smart, and decent girls about future travel plans together. Was I a lucky man or what? This seemed like a dream too good to be true.

I had never planned to hook up with women, especially with three, but certainly, I was in no danger; the possible expansion of relations with these women was an incredible proposition; what was the downside, I was saying to myself.

Ina was meeting my eye contact, and I would say there was a considerable spark there, at least from my perspective. Ina asked me to dance and, wrapped herself around me and whispered in my ear that I was an interesting old man. I was enjoying this attention immensely, and of course, my wanker was hard as a rock, and Ina was enjoying this as much as me. Missy and Cherri commented that we should get a room, and Ina just laughed and said we will see.

That night, **Feb 19**, back at the Tombstone Lodge, we were all quite drunk, and after hot tubing, we all fell into our beds and slept. In the morning, I had coffee, kiwi fruit salad, boiled eggs, and toast made for everyone. As I always carried my smoothie ingredients with me, I made a double batch and offered that to the girls as well; they did not know that there was a good slosh of vodka included!

Watching women with hangovers revive themselves, shower, and come alive is a pleasure for an old man. We decided to stay another night, relax, revive with the hot tub, and then later find a pub and just have one or two beers with supper. After Ina, the last to get up, finished showering and came to eat, she surprisingly said, 'Where did this all come from?' Missy just pointed at me and smiled.

We toured around Picton and found a nice secluded beach to lie in the sun. Missy, Cherri, and Ina all looked gorgeous with their bikinis on, and someone had to spread the suntan lotion on!

Ina wondered how an old man could have such a body as mine; I said, 'It's just the genes.' Later, we found a pub that served all-you-can-eat fresh seafood, gorged ourselves, and I treated the girls to the meal. We got an early night, and the atmosphere with bunking in four bunk beds was interesting, to say the least, for an old man. The lodge provided breakfast the next day, and Ina asked what happened to the cook. Was he on strike? We all laughed.

We packed up the SUV, and I was the driver today. We continued south on Highway One with Hanmer Springs as our destination. The drive along the coast is as good a scenic route as you can find anywhere in the world. We stopped at Kaikoura, a gorgeous seaside town, for lunch.

After lunch, we continued on to Hanmer Hot Springs. We knew it was a tourist destination, so it was likely costly to stay, but the hot springs were on our list. We managed to find a bed and breakfast at a reasonable price with 3 beds and a nice hot tub area with a fire pit. We settled in and had some soup and sandwiches, the old guy cooking.

We hit the Hot Springs and were not disappointed. With Kaikora being a tourist destination, the nightlife was lively, and we enjoyed some local musicians and local brewed beers. Ina was the spark plug to get us going; Missy, Cherri, me, and Ina all danced together. I felt very lucky to be hooked up with these girls; they were very lively.

Like anywhere in the world, you cannot escape from the odd drunk when at a public pub. A guy was dancing with us, which is no big deal today, but he was trying to pick up Ina and asked if I was her father. We tried to ignore him, but he followed us to our table, and we had to tell him to bugger off.

Ina went to the washroom, and I noticed after she went down the hallway, the drunk went that way also. I waited a reasonable time for Ina to return, and when I thought it was too long, I went to investigate.

The drunk was preventing Ina from passing through and talking to her. I approached and yelled at him to leave her alone. The drunk turned and told me to bugger off and took a wild haymaker swing at me.

Having been in bar fights before, I ducked under his wild punch and delivered an uppercut to his midsection. I got lucky and hit his solar plexus just right, and he doubled over and was gasping for air. I grabbed his head and brought up my knee as hard as I could, and his head snapped back, and he was against the wall. I followed up with as good a right punch as I could and landed square on his chin. He slid down the wall dazed, and I could have continued to pummel him, but that is not my nature.

A big, burly bartender grabbed me from behind in a bear hug, and I just relaxed. Ina was crying and told the bartenders what had happened, and the guy holding me said in his native Kiwi, 'You bonked him good, boyo, good on ya!!' The bartenders had the drunk with his arms behind his back and were taking him out the back door.

A barmaid had taken Ina into the ladies' washroom, so I returned to my table. Missy and Chrissie asked what was going on because two policemen had arrived. I sat down and explained what had happened, and Missy and Chrissie went to the ladies washroom. They all came back, and Ina was fine but very angry. She explained that she had a brown belt in Jujitsu but had never used it and was ashamed that she was unable to react quickly enough.

One policeman came back and asked Ina if she could explain what happened and eventually asked if she wished to press charges. Ina declined as he had not touched her; he was just in her way. The policeman assured us the drunk would spend the night in the drunk tank and not bother us again.

Missy and Chrissie had invited two English blokes to our table, and they were chatting with them. The big bartender came to our table and suggested they did not have any chance to provide some punishment to the drunk as he was still dazed and gasping for air, so they left him.

Ina was upset and wanted to leave. Missy and Chrissie said they would stay as they wanted to chat with the Limy blokes. I suggested to Ina I would walk her back to our B&B. Ina was pleased I was accompanying her, and once outside, she put her arm through mine and thanked me for my help. I explained that I do not have any martial arts, but I said bar fights are often free for all melees, and I had been in a few. She calmed down and expressed that there was lots more to this old man she was walking with than meets the eye.

The B&B was not far, and when we arrived, Ina wanted to take a dip in the hot tub and relax, so we both changed and had a beer in the tub. After a nice soak, we were chatting, and Ina was looking into my eyes; I assumed with a desire for more than chatting. We got out, and Ina told me to shower first.

I was soaping myself down, and Ina opened the shower door and suggested she could soap my back; she was completely naked, and what a sight. I turned to her and stood there shocked, and the obvious happened as I felt a very strong stirring. I was trying to speak, and Ina said, 'Shut up and kiss me.' We were trying to shower by kissing and touching each other, and finally scrambled to one of the beds and fell onto it. The sex was incredible for me, and by Ina's sounds and actions, she was enjoying it as much as I was.

We lay entwined together, and I was exhausted. Ina was asking me many things about my youth and my life, and I was doing the same. It was like the beginning of a love story, I thought, how this could be happening to a seventy-five-year-old man and a thirty-two-year-old beautiful Swedish bombshell.

After a while, the realization that I had this incredible woman in my arms, things began to stir again, and we had a second incredible lovemaking session, this time, taking our time and enjoying everything to its fullest. We fell asleep entangled together, and that was difficult for me as I had been single for a long time and not sleeping with any woman.

We woke up in the morning, and Missy and Chrissie were not in the room. I got up and, made some coffee and asked Ina if she wanted to shower. She got up, led me back to the bed, and started kissing me all over so we had another round of slow and incredible sex; she was no stranger to this. After we showered, I got the breakfast provided, and we were relaxing and lying on our bed in the room. Missy and Chrissie arrived back and took one look at me, and Ina and Missy said, 'You guys look like you enjoyed your night together.' Ina just smiled and kissed me.

Missy and Chrissie showered, dipped in the hot tub, and had breakfast. I commented that they had to have slept somewhere, and Chrissie just moved her finger across her mouth; they were not telling us anything.

We packed up and continued south on Highway One. It was **Feb 20** when we arrived in Christchurch. We found a supermarket and replenished our cooler supplies. We found our way to Shamarra Alpacas and toured the farm. They produced the best wool to use for sweaters, mitts, socks, and toques. The scenery with the mountains in the west and the ocean in the east was often breathtaking.

The side trip to the Alpacas farm was not a great distance but quite mountainous and slow, so we booked a B&B in Christchurch. We chose the Jailhouse Accommodation, which was an old jail converted into a B&B, complete with fake prisoners and bars on the windows. It was unique, with various areas preserved with authentic jailhouse inmate mannequins, furniture, toilets, etc.

Ina and I chose our own cell, and Missy and Cherrie were not surprised at this. We spent a few hours on the beach and then found a seafood restaurant and had fresh fish with beer. We got an early night compared to the last couple, and Missy and Chrissie wished us a good night of sleeping, Missy winking at me.

Ina and I were talking about our families; her parents were both very busy. Her father was a criminal lawyer in a firm, and her mother was an editor. I described my farm background, and I told her I had written a story about the Family Farm history.

We enjoyed the best breakfast of all to date with kiwi fruit salad, bacon, and eggs with toast, orange juice, and coffee. The proprietors were a great couple and fun to chat with. We broke out of jail at about 9 am on Feb 22, traveling south along the coast.

The scenery is some of the best I have experienced; we had many stops to stretch and take pictures. We arrived at Gore and looked up a sheep farm tour just south of Gore. We had not booked ahead for a room anywhere. At the South Sheep Farm, we had a tour and a sheep herding demonstration with a sheepdog. The sheep farm owner had a friend he suggested we stay with at a B&B

called the Reservation and booked two rooms as Ina and I would bunk together.

It was the most beautiful B&B we had seen, with more or less a farm atmosphere that was well-kept. The rooms were modern, and we were tired from a long day, so we settled in our rooms, and Ina and I enjoyed an active evening again. The next morning, breakfast was delicious and as much as you could eat.

We carried on heading for Queenstown in the mountains. Arriving there about noon, We found the accommodations expensive but we settled on finding the Judge and Jury Farm Retreat. It was on the way for our travel the next day and as picturesque as you will ever find. The owners were as accommodating as any we had, and the farm hiking trails and scenery were breathtaking.

Ina wanted to hike with me alone, and we found a place to cozy up and get naked in the wild!! I found her to have a very voracious sexual appetite, which I had managed to satisfy.

Breakfast was scrumptious with home-style cooking, and we carried on through mountain highways and back to the East Coast. It was so beautiful, and we had many stops to stretch, snack, and take photos. We arrived back at Christchurch and chose the Jailhouse B&B because we had enjoyed it there before.

"Arrival New Zealand"

After a night in jail, with a great breakfast again, we were off the Pickton to catch the ferry back to Wellington. The ferry ride was not as nice as the previous one, and the weather was pouring rain, and the water was much rougher.

After arriving in Wellington, we settled on the Cambridge Hotel, as it was old, picturesque, and cheap. We had a shared room with four bunks, so I thought I had a night off from sleeping with Ina. Missy and Cherrie advised that they were going shopping and would leave the two lovebirds alone for a few hours.

Breakfast was not as big as some of the others, but the standard Kiwi fruit salad was great. We got an early start as it was 7 hours to Auckland; we arrived on **Feb 25**. We had been on the road for sixteen days.

Missy and Cherri were discussing their finances on the drive to Auckland and were pleasantly surprised how shared traveling costs are beneficial. We checked the SUV in, and that took a bit more of all of our funds, but split four ways for almost half the trip, at least the part with Ina included; it was very reasonable.

We checked out air flight costs to Sydney for the next day for $130 one way, so we all booked on the same flight and then found rooms near the airport for $101/night. We booked 2 rooms, ate leftover food from our cooler, and there was a nice lounge at the hotel. At the lounge, I sold the cooler for a round of drinks. We were tired from the day's drive and settled in for the night.

Ina was active as ever when we got in our room, and after we had relaxing sex, we were lying and talking. She was expressing her luck at finding our group to travel with. I asked her if she was having concerns about sleeping with an old man, and her reaction was to proceed to show me how much she enjoyed my company. We never discussed money; Ina paid her way, and I paid mine.

We had some time to ourselves on the trip with Missy and Cherri, but much of it involved them, and did not have a lot of private conversations. She said she could not wait to get me alone when Missy and Cherri returned to England. She was not upset with traveling with them but thought we would have fewer issues with food, rooms, and our choice of what to do. I mirrored her thoughts and told her before I met her on the ferry, I was fine with traveling with them, but when you started traveling with us, I was having such romantic and erotic thoughts about this bombshell Swedish gal.

I told her that I do not think she knows how sexy she is. I watch men looking at you every day and know their thoughts. I laughed and said many of them must think you are traveling with your father. She was not concerned and advised that I am a decent, sexy man myself, and she is quite happy with my company.

Chapter 3
"New Zealand to Australia"

I had contacted Ted and Tessie Cross in Sydney before I left on my trip. I had not specified what my date of arrival in Sydney might be, so I called them to advise that we would be flying over from Auckland tomorrow. Tessie asked what 'we' meant, and I told her about my travelling companions and where we had been. Tessie said, 'You old man, what do you think you are doing?' I said, 'enjoying myself.'

She was happy to pick us up at the airport, and she said her house was our house and she would manage somehow. Tessie and Ted are in their eighties, and I was concerned about being a burden to them and told her so. She said, 'Nonsense, it will liven up our boring lives.' I thanked her and advised her that she would find an old man travelling with three beautiful ladies, so she should be able to pick us out.

The next morning, we had a small breakfast at the hotel, nothing like the B&Bs we had experienced. We caught a cab to the airport and boarded our flight as scheduled, arriving in Sydney at noon on **February 26, 2026.**

Tessie was at the arrival doors, and she was smiling ear to ear and gave me a big hug; then she hugged each of my companions. She commented that when my brother arrived in **1967**, he was with her son Eddie and not three beautiful ladies.

The girls were quite taken with her welcome and even more so when we arrived at her home. Tessie was a ball of fire with a barrage of questions about Les, me, my trip, and the girls with me. She was not sure of sleeping arrangements, and Ina politely said 'I will sleep with the old man if I can.' Tessie was laughing so hard it was infectious, and we all laughed till tears flowed.

We all sat down on her patio to enjoy the iced tea and snacks she had laid out. Tessie was so curious about how we met up, and the girls filled her in on the details. She looked at me a couple of times and said, 'You are one lucky old man; I hope you are not sleeping with all three.' That brought another round of gut-laughing, and we were in for a great visit.

Ted arrived home from shopping; he had gone for beer. He had an idea what to expect from the phone call the night before but was dumbfounded how an old geezer could be travelling with three chicks as hot as these. Another round of laughing, and he offered cold beer and saluted to good times and life.

Tessie had a supper planned of roast lamb and all the trimmings that went with it. The conversation was nonstop, and I was thankful to sit and enjoy without much input. I like to talk, but I like to listen more. Tessie had stories of her own travels to many places and Canada, where she visited our farm when I was about 13 or 14.

Tessie and Ted were such fantastic hosts; it is never as good in any hotel or B&B, no matter how accommodating the owner is, compared to being in someone's home. We chatted till the next day and finally hit the sack. Tessie was tsking about the sleeping arrangements, and the best part was Missy and Cherri had couches.

Breakfast was the start of another day of visiting and feast after feast. We thought we were going to bust our guts with food, drinks and laughter from the Australia-style hospitality. Tessie had a number of friends who came by for drinks and chats with this unusual foursome of guests. I was given the gears by a number of Aussies who thought I was some kind of Superman; someone had leaked that I was sleeping with all of them.

I had mentioned to Ted that I was interested in something like a VW travel van or a similar small motor home that would accommodate four. One of Ted's friends had a couple of vehicles he had in mind, one that sounded really promising.

The partying carried on late into the second night as word got around to come for a few beers and meet Les's brother and his harem. There was much slapping on the back, as this seemed to be an Aussie custom when emphasizing my plight of travelling with these ladies. Ina thought it was hilarious and, at one point, was sitting on my lap and was telling a number of Aussie chaps that he is mine and only mine.

I have learned with age and experience that I need to control my drinking, but the Aussie crowd was infectious, and there were so many cheers like 'Get on the grog' or 'Get a black dog up ya.' I was plastered by the end of the night. Missy, Cherri and Ina were like me, but especially Chrissie, who was passed out on the floor in one corner of the room.

The next day, we were all sporting hangovers; coffee and a hearty breakfast were doing wonders, but in my experience, time and lots of water are the only answer.

Ted's friend arrived at Ted's place driving a 2010 VW camper van. He said, 'Look her over, bucko; she is a beaut.' The VW was in decent shape but had 150,000 kilometers. It had been looked after pretty well, I could tell, but driving it proved a different story as it had been parked a few years.

I wanted a vehicle that could go across the outback and not leave me stranded. My assessment indicated it needed tires, brakes, alignment, and possibly a motor and transmission assessment. Ted's friend said I could take it for $2500 Aussie dollars, which is almost par with the Canadian dollar. I paid him $2000, and now I had a money pit.

Ted's friend knew a mechanics shop that would do all I wanted and at a decent rate. We popped over to this shop, and after his estimate and much haggling, we settled on a maximum of $3000 dollars, and she would get me to Darwin. This mechanic was from Darwin and assured me if I limp the beast into Darwin, I would get my money back.

We had a week to kill to wait for repairs to be completed, so Ted and Tessie insisted we stay with them, and they could tour us around.

On February 29, Tessie self-appointed herself as our guide, and we travelled north to Brisbane. I drove as Tessie was in her mid-eighties, and she gave a guided tour as we drove up the Sunshine Coast. She insisted on a five-star hotel on the beach and was paying for everything. We were all a little taken aback by this arrangement as we had been paying our way.

We had beautiful rooms and an oceanfront view, but it did not feel right. We enjoyed ourselves; the beach was great, the hotel top-notch, but we all realized that Tessie was just that much older than even me, and we all wanted to return to Sydney. I think Tessie sensed this and was happy to get back to her home and Ted.

Back in Sydney, Missy and Cherri took me and Ina out for a chat about travel plans. Missy and Cherri wished to rent their own car again and split on their own. They did not want to hang around Sydney; they were very appreciative of Tessie and Ted's hospitality but decided to continue on their own.

They also thought the VW van would be great for Ina and me, but it would be crowded with four, and where would everyone sleep? I did not disagree with them, and although Ina was unhappy to see them plan to leave, she knew they were right.

We took Tessie and Ted out for supper on us, and it was a fitting farewell for Missy and Cherri also. Ted gave them an old cooler, as they told him about my knowledge of teaching them travelling with water, drinks and snacks and got them a great deal on a rental.

Ina called her parents in Stockholm, Sweden and updated her on her trip with three other people in New Zealand, flying to Sydney and meeting my friends and our trip up the Sunshine Coast.

She explained about the plans for the girls to go on their own and my purchase of the VW van and plans to travel with just her through Australia. She came to me and asked if I would speak with her father. He was very concerned for Ina and asked my age and background. When I told him my age, he was confused because I think he thought I was much younger.

He had little choice but to wish us good luck and please look after their daughter. Ina was back on the phone and related what I had done at the bar in New Zealand, and I think they possibly had some assurance that Ina was in good hands. Ina was very straightforward with her mother and told her, of course, she was sleeping with me; her mother said to be careful, in other words, not to get pregnant. Ina told her my friend Tessie had grilled her about this also.

The next morning, Missy and Cherri were off with hugs all around and promises to keep in touch. Later that day, I visited the mechanic who was fixing my VW, and he surprised me by telling me he would be finished the next day, three days early.

He did not have to rebuild the engine; compression in each cylinder was good, and he flushed it, set the valves, and changed the transmission fluid also. It had new rubber all around, and two spares with rims, and he had done an alignment. I asked him to check out the stove, fridge, and all electrical inside the camper, and he said, 'Already done bucko, she is all good.'

Ina and I had a nice, quiet supper with Tessie and Ted, and at noon the next day, Ted and I went and picked up my VW.

On March 2, we said our goodbyes to Tessie and Ted, packed our stuff in the van, and were off on our own. The van was a standard, but Ina was experienced with shifting a standard and was looking forward to driving. The van was no powerhouse, but with the engine maintenance and a new carburetor, it scooted along pretty good, and mileage was great.

The 2 extra tires with rims from the mechanic were tied on the rear carrier. The fridge was cool, and we stopped to do a major shop at a supermarket for all the foods we initially needed and would complete what we needed as we traveled. The van had a 20-gallon water tank for dishes and cooking, and I bought a five-gallon water jug for spare water. We packed bottled water to drink.

Ina was so excited and impressed with my knowledge and planning for this journey. She thought I was a genius, but I told her it was old hat as I had done this so much.

She laughed at my list that I was in the habit of making when traveling like this. She was curious where we could stop to christen the bed; I kidded her that she was a sex maniac.

We travelled for six hours and arrived at Mallacoota, which is about halfway to Melbourne. We booked at the Mallacoota campground, parked our van in our spot, and started to get used to all the van's various gadgets, the stove, the pop-up roof bed, and all the amenities it had.

Ina was fascinated that I knew how to unlatch and pop up the roof that exposed the bed. Ina asked me 'where is the bathroom' I laughed and pointed to the washroom and shower building across the road; I told her I picked this spot as it was close to the washhouse. She was giggling and quite excited to try out the bed.

We both needed a shower, and she was not impressed that we could not shower together. I finished my shower and had tea, soup, and a sandwich made when she got back. She kissed me and advised me that the sandwich had to wait as she could not wait any longer to try the bed.

Since it was her first time in a camper van, she was constantly giggling and finding the experience a lot of fun. She asked where the bedding and comforter came from, and I explained I bought them in Sydney; they were on my list.

Our sex became quite energetic, and the van was rocking pretty good, which only caused more giggling from Ina. After we relaxed, she realized that we were not that far from other campers, and there was more giggling. She was impressed that I had warm, wet face cloths to wash our privates after sex. She asked if I had packed these or where I got them. I said, 'I bought them in Sydney;

it was on my list,' and I soaked them in my shower. We had our supper and crawled back into bed.

We slept like logs, as it had been a long day and an energetic night before supper. The weather was cool at night, and I knew we might not need another comforter or a warm blanket, as Ina was like an oven, and this I was not used to.

I was awakened by Ina, who proceeded to want sex, and I was not one to dissuade her. After rocking the van again, Ina curled up beside me and was sleeping again.

I got up and cooked boiled eggs and pancakes with coffee and fresh fruit salad. When Ina smelled the cooking, she crawled down from our bed and sat naked, eating her breakfast. I thought I had died and gone to heaven. What a trip this was going to be with this woman I was getting very comfortable with.

The van packed up very easily and quickly, so we were on our way headed for Melbourne, arriving on **March 4, 2026.** The drive was six hours, so we found the Discovery Parks campsite we had chosen to set up and just relaxed at the pool and planned to see various attractions the next day or two.

I advised Ina I had discovered four fold-down stabilizer legs on the four corners of the van to stop the rocking when moving around in the van or when having sex. She was eager to try it out, and it was way less rocking!!

This activity pattern of ours was very pleasing, to say the least. I was still able to manage the travel and sex, but with my age, I was looking ahead and wondering how long I could sustain this level of activity.

Ina was such a pleasure to be around. She was smart and thoughtful, appreciated my knowledge and experience, had funds, could drive, liked to plan ahead, and had a great sense of fun and humor. She was sexy as hell, so what was my problem?

She drove some on the open highway portions but preferred I drive when nearing and in the cities. I guess an old man thinks differently along the lines that if it seems too good to be true, it likely is not true. I shelved these thoughts and decided to 'enjoy the ride, old man, as long as it lasts.'

Today, after a salad, cereal, and coffee breakfast, we checked out various tours that included many attractions, but these cost a lot of money. We had our own wheels and could choose what we wanted.

We drove downtown and first visited the Melbourne Skydeck for a stunning view of the city. We continued with a walking tour of Finders Street, Melbourne Lane, Federation Square, old Melbourne Gaol, and AC/DC Lane.

We had munched on croissants and beer, and as we were tired, we returned to the Discovery Park campsite. We showered, and I cooked up a soup and sandwich, which we enjoyed with beer. We went to relax by the pool and were happy to go to bed early. Ina surprised me and went immediately to sleep.

The next morning, I was awakened by a rambunctious Ina with her hunger for sex. After the invigorating session, I cooked some bacon and eggs. We showered and packed up as our day's plan was to visit the Great Ocean Road, including the twelve apostles and the Great Otway National Park.

That took up most of our day, and we continued in the direction of Grampians National Park. We choose the MacKenzie Falls campground for our night stay. After a quick snack, we went on a hike to the falls; I packed a little backpack with some soap and a towel. My fanny pack was always with me with our passports, money, and credit cards. Campgrounds are pretty safe here, much like Canada, I told Ina, but one never knows; thieves are worldwide.

The falls were really nice, but signs indicated that no bathing was allowed. Since there were no showers at the campground, we needed to bathe, so we found a secluded pool and stripped down to bathe. Ina saw the opportunity for, guess what, 'sex,' and we were exposed but enjoyed it immensely and then bathed in the cold water.

There were kangaroos, Wallabies, and a few koala bears on our hike, both to the falls and back to camp. We were beat and settled in for the night. The weather had been fantastic, hot and dry; from the time we left Sydney, we were in the late part of their summer. The nights can be cool as it is along the south coast because there are ocean breezes that come inland.

There seemed to be some mosquitoes, flies, and bugs, but they were manageable; I was always thinking of scorpions and snakes but had not seen any so far.

On March 7, we packed up and headed south to the coast again, with no specific destination in mind, maybe Port Macdonnell, as there was a penguin colony there. Traveling along the coast, it is nice to have the sea breeze blowing; it helps with the heat. We were looking for a secluded place to park, boondocking instead of staying at a campsite. This is not allowed in most places, but it is possible for single nights.

Near Port MacDonnell, we found a beach area with a hill separating us from the highway and set up camp. I cooked a steak supper with baked potatoes, canned green peas, sour cream, and a mushroom/butter sauce. Ina ate like she was starving and gave me a reward for cooking supper with an after-supper dessert Ina style!!

We went to the beach for a swim, and I had my little pack with soap and a towel. We tucked in for the night, and it seemed to be blowing more, and off to the south, the sea looked angry.

Conversation with Ina was nonstop. We talked about each other's upbringing, which was so different. She was born and raised in Stockholm and spent all her school and university years there. She graduated from university with a commerce degree and was apprenticing as a financial advisor. She worked her way up the ladder to have her own group of investors she had gathered from relatives, friends, and some from the firm she was with. Her group of investors were very happy with her management of their funds, as returns were good for them.

She had a relationship for about ten years and found herself and her partner in a rut; she wanted to break out from her partner. She decided to take a leave of absence from her position to travel, and an associate would manage her group of investors. After much research, she chose New Zealand as her first destination.

She did not have hitchhiking experience, and she had a couple of rides that scared her. Consequently, when she was talking with me on the ferry ride, she felt immediately safe and at ease of feelings.

Her interest in me was not as a future partner; she wanted safety and thought our trio would benefit us all. She did initially think one of the girls was my daughter. From then till now, lying in the camper, she reflected that from an initial joining up of travelers to all the experiences we had, then our plans to travel together, just us two, has filled her dreams of this trip beyond her wildest expectations. She appreciated my standing up for her, respecting her wishes, and not pushing or suggesting anything she did not want to do.

My history is a long story compared to Ina's, and I tried to chronologically tell her my history of growing up on a farm in central Alberta. I explained my career and some of my work experiences.

I explained my two marriages, my three children, and their history. I reviewed my current life, where I had sold my home and was now homeless, downsized everything I owned, stored what I wanted and could keep in a big cargo trailer, and decided to go where the wind blew me.

I explained that my brother's experiences with all kinds of people to hook up with as travel mates were a large part of his success for not only his safety but companionship. I told her I was so surprised to have Missy and Chrissie's choice to travel with me.

I showed her my story again that I wrote about this long journey of his and my desire to try to retrace some of this exceptional trip. We could often talk for hours as soul mates and were so interested in each other.

In the camper that night, we were recalling our stories to each other over the past week. We had learned much more than when traveling with the two girls. She would not say she loved me but had a tear in her eye as she kissed me and was soon asleep in my arms.

I really felt I was in a difficult situation. I wanted to travel with Ina to India, but I was projecting ahead to future years, and with my current nomadic lifestyle and no place to call home, how would this affect our relationship after traveling? It was a dilemma where I currently thought I was one lucky old redneck farm boy, but what was to come?

The morning brought a fresh desire from Ina for our morning sex. I made my smoothie; I needed the nourishment from it with our frequent carnal activity. We packed up and found the penguin colony. The hiking on the cliffs was tough on an old man; Ina was always ahead and finding a new path and challenge.

On March 8, we continued along the coast without any specific destination other than Adelaide. A couple of hours down the coast, we decided to stay at Long Beach. There were tons of vehicles parked along the beach, and asking a couple of people who apparently were camping, we were told it was ok, just not more than a day or two. We found a supermarket to stock up on food we needed, got gas, and filled the propane tank and our water supply.

We found and toured the Rancho Los Cerritos. A group of ladies with the owner's wife were having a knitting bee. They were so friendly, and the owner's wife, Melanie, asked me and my daughter to join her for supper at her house. We went to the beach for most of the afternoon and swam in the ocean to wash ourselves. When we arrived for supper, Melanie had a spread laid out that would feed an army, and the beer was cold.

Her husband, Jack, asked how a father and daughter trip was going, and Ina was giggling and explained how we met and what our plans were. Melanie was sitting there shocked, and she said well then, I suppose you sleep together in that little van and Ina just laughed.

We had a great night and drove along the coast till we found a secluded spot to park for the night. Ina was apologetic that her monthly was happening, and I was given a much-needed rest.

Ina seemed a little quiet and had a concerned look on her face, so I asked what was bothering her. She said when Melanie and she were walking in the garden, Melanie asked what her and my intentions were as a couple.

Ina explained she had not thought about it much and was just going with the flow. Melanie said well then, you better not get pregnant. I could see her dilemma because we had never talked about or used protection during sex.

I put her mind to rest, advising her that my tubes were tied after my last son was born and 'I was shooting blanks.' She laughed at that phrase but told me she was not on the pill, and it surprised her when Melanie had brought it up, but it made her think about it.

Morning brought a surprise storm coming in from the south; summer was more or less officially over here, so this was welcome to all the farmers in this southern coastal region. This storm did not last long and was not really severe. We drove through it, arriving in Adelaide at about noon **on March 9;** the Adelaide region is quite dry as it does not receive much annual rainfall.

I splurged for a couple of tours, partly because we had not taken any tours, but also because from here going north, we would be in the outback and little of this type of attractions.

We went on a Dolphin cruise, which included a fish meal on the boat. Then we went to the National Wine Center of Australia, as Adelaide was famous for its wineries. We camped at the Big 4 Port Willunga tourist park as it was cheap and had showers.

We did a little shopping; I realized that I had not offered Ina the chance to shop. She expressed that she was not a big shopper and was concerned about gathering too much stuff. She was planning ahead, and I suggested when we get to Darwin and I sell the van, she can pack up what is extra and ship it home.

We had a quiet night around the pool and chatting with other travelers. I noticed that when we were traveling with Missy and Cherri, there always seemed to be more of a partying atmosphere. Just me and Ina, I felt like less of the partying desires.

Lying in our van bed, Ina was apprehensive about our route through the outback. Would our van be ok? What about water and food? I explained that I expected the highway would be much better than 1967 when my brother traveled this route.

On Google Maps, it was only fifteen hours to Alice Springs and another fifteen hours to Darwin. I was not suggesting we travel straight thru; I was thinking of taking a week or more to get to Darwin.

I suggested we go to a supermarket before leaving Adelaide to stock up on water and food. I would look for a mechanic to do a once-over of the van's motor, transmission, and tires, essentially checking all the running gear.

The campground manager knew a friend from an automotive shop and called him. He would take us first thing in the morning and check out what we wanted. After a quiet night with Ina, we woke the next morning, had a swim and shower, and went to the mechanic's shop. I explained that I thought the van had some drive shaft noise.

Most everything was ok, but he suggested that the drive shaft needed two steady bearings, considering where we were going. He suggested the ones on it were original and had no lubricant, and they had a play in them.

He also suggested changing the differential gear oil as it was old. They had found the parts in Adelaide and would have us on the road by day's end. We picked up the van at closing, and we booked another night at the Big 4 Willunga Park and took our beach things to lie in the sun and relax. Ina was happy to do some shopping, mostly souvenirs for her family back home in Sweden.

The mechanic had topped up our propane and filled our water tank. He suggested I take spare spark plugs, a fan belt, and a spare oil filter and oil. He had changed the oil as I had told him about the engine flush; he was a gem thinking of all these things.

I was feeling quite happy that Ina had expressed her concerns, which instigated the mechanic's work on the van. She was exhibiting survival thoughts, which were beneficial for both of us, considering where we were going. She was having some difficulties with a toothache, which was minor at the time.

On March 11, we were on the road early and followed the A1 highway, arriving at Port Augusta at about noon. The route followed Spencer Bay, and the countryside was still fertile and green. It was starting to have much less vegetation, and it was warmer.

We checked into the shoreline Caravan Park. The pool and washrooms were excellent; I was pleasantly surprised that Ina informed me she was cooking. She said she had been watching me do the cooking and wanted to try. She made a delicious supper but wanted me to cook the steaks. I sat back, sucking on a beer, and enjoyed every moment of watching her busy cooking.

We had an early night, and Ina curled up around me; she was sleeping quickly and was like an oven. I had all the windows open, and it was not hot, but I was wondering what was coming in the weeks ahead.

We were up early and on the road, continuing onto Highway A87 with Ina driving. We traveled five hours to Coober Pedy. The countryside changed to sparse greenery, to no green, and more or less desert. You could feel the heat, and with no air conditioning, it was a sign of things to come. We were wearing shorts and T-shirts with sandals.

Coober Pedy is small and has opal fields nearby. We toured the Underground Motel, which lives up to its name with rooms underground and thus providing built-in air conditioning. Ina was so enthralled with the underground hotel idea that she insisted we stop at another one, the Radeka Downunder Motel, and she booked a room, her treat.

She said we would never have this chance again, and the price was reasonable. We had a few beers at a local pub, and I was given directions on where to go for the best opal mooching on the Coober opal fields. A guy at the bar warned us to keep an eye out for scorpions; I was not sure if he was kidding, but I planned to heed his advice.

Our night in the underground motel room was a fantastic experience. I felt a little claustrophobic, and other than some minor fan noise, there was a dead silence once in our room. It had all the amenities any motel has. The walls and roof were solid rock, and there was no shoring of the walls or roof. With my engineering background, I was expressing my nervousness, but it just took some getting used to.

Ina was like a kid in a playhouse, and since her monthly had passed, she was eager to try out sex in an underground motel. She was quite vocal and giggling and laughing. She took pictures of us sitting on our beds; we only had towels wrapped around ourselves, and she had to go to the surface to send photos to her parents.

There was breakfast provided, the fruit salad and a bannock type of flat bread with boiled eggs and great coffee. The owner, Marty, had packed our lunch in a little cooler, which was not included in our room costs, and wished us luck opal mooching. Ina was complaining that her toothache was worse, and I gave her a Motrin for the pain.

The drive to the opal fields was short, and we approached another couple who parked beside us. They had been mooching before and went to their favorite spot and showed us what to look for.

We mooched for about four hours and were rewarded with about ten smaller opals and one long oval-shaped Ina found. She let out a yelp when she found it, and the couple with us said they had never found one that size; it was about one-half inch long, and the guy said to get it cut, trimmed, and polished and have it set in a ring or have a hole made to wear it just as is for a necklace. Ina was over the moon as she said she would get it made for her and her mother into matching rings.

It was quite hot and we had sweated all day, so the little cooler that the underground motel guy packed for us with our lunch surprised us with a six-pack of beer in the bottom. It was just the reward for our efforts, and we shared our beers with the other couple.

We made arrangements to meet the couple, Allan and Char, for supper together at the local opal bullshitting pub. Back at the underground motel, the owner was laughing at us and our luck. He said he knew we would return for another night; the lunch and beer were his bribes. He was very impressed with Ina's opal and was rubbing his hands together with a big grin.

We booked another night and enjoyed a much-needed shower. Ina was so overjoyed with her opal find that she declared we had to celebrate and proceeded to show me her enthusiasm in the shower and then in bed!!!

The night at the local opal bullshitting bar was a blast. There had to be about twenty people who were wagering bets on who found the best opal that day. Our motel owner was there, and since he had seen Ina's opal, he was wagering heavily with a bunch of the locals that this greenhorn bombshell Swedish chick would be the winner.

Apparently, it is a custom that has been going on for years, and that day's winner gets a t-shirt with the Coober Pedy logo. Ina won hands down, and the opal found its way around to all and the oohs and aaws were genuine, as it was definitely a beauty.

The catch for winning this t-shirt is that the winner must change right there in the bar. Ina did not disappoint anyone; she stripped off her blouse, and she was not wearing a bra; she trilled the whole crowd. There was much cheering and back-slapping. It seems an Aussie custom for a lucky guy like me.

Marty, the motel owner, was collecting his winnings, and most of the locals were cat calling him about a setup. We said nothing; the bullshit and consuming of many beers carried on till closing time.

We arrived back at our underground room, fell into bed, and slept like logs. The silence in the room was an eerie feeling.

In the morning, we were a little out of sorts from the night's activities. We showered and were treated to a full breakfast as Marty said he did well with his wagering last night, and it was the least he could do. Ina was having considerable pain from her toothache. I asked about a dentist, and Marty said old Fred pulls my teeth.

He charged us half price for our room and sent us on our way with a cold six-pack of beer. Ina hugged him, and he told her to take it easy on the old man. She said that he needs to take it easy on her. Everyone was laughing, and we had experienced some true Aussie outback hospitality.

We filled up with gas and started the drive from Coober Pedy to Alice Springs. It is a bleak and lonesome landscape, with little to see and very few stops, with only little hamlets or just a trailer or two.

The temperature was over 100 F, and we had the windows down but sweating in the dry heat. The van was purring along just like it loved it, and I was so glad we had repaired the steady bearings and differential gear oils. Getting stranded in the desert would not be fun.

We arrived on **March 14** at the border between South and North Australia, which has a rest stop. The showers and BBQ areas are free, and we enjoyed this luxury after many hot hours of traveling.

The camping was free, so we decided to stay the night. The night cools down considerably in the desert, but you need to stay up till the cool-down starts. I cooked a light supper of fish and a salad; we enjoyed the cold beer Marty had provided

I checked the van over for engine oil level, the transmission fluid level, the coolant fluid level, and the fan belt condition. The engine had not overheated, so we were good. The older VW vans that were air-cooled would likely be overheating much easier.

I was telling Ina how the highway is a paved surface now, unlike 1967 when my two brothers traveled this same route. Chris recalled the gravel was quite abrasive and wore the tires down quickly. They ran out of spares and, at one point, cut down saplings and stuffed them in between the rim and the rubber to get to the next stop where they could buy tires.

The 1960's VW van my brother's had was air-cooled, and Chris said they had overheating problems many days. The three spares I had were likely not required.

There are still warnings that during the rainy season, the highway can be flooded in some areas, but for the most part, the highway now has drainage capabilities from one side to the other.

I helped Ina prepare supper. I built a fire in a BBQ pit and showed her how to prepare baked potatoes in tinfoil and put them in the fire for an hour, and then I cooked the steaks on the hot coals. She was impressed with my cooking the steaks on an open fire and how the taste was delicious. I told her stories Les and Chris had related about their travel thru this same route and their difficulties.

Ike's Travels

The boon docking here let you choose where to park, it was not organized; it was a free for all. We chose an out-of-the-way location and set up, but Ina's tooth was bothering her badly.

I asked to see which tooth. I looked at it and felt it; it was loose and did not look good, as the area was red and likely had some infection. I asked her if she would let me pull it, and she gave me a very confused and scared look. I explained that it may be days before we get to a dentist, and it should come out now.

She reluctantly agreed, and I brought out my small bag of tools. I chose smaller channel lock pliers. Ina was very scared, and I got the channel lock on the right setting and locked on the tooth. I asked her to squeeze a beer bottle in each hand. I said, 'Squeeze hard' and tightening the channel lock and pulling at the same time, the tooth popped out and I grabbed a face cloth, and she stuffed that in her mouth. She was grimacing in pain, but it passed quite quickly. I asked her to rinse her mouth with some whisky a couple of times and gave her two Motrin.

I got her out for a walk to take her mind off the tooth, and we settled in for the night. During the night, I heard the yapping of coyotes and dingoes. After it cooled down, it was quite comfortable, especially with Ina as my oven.

I woke up and made coffee and toast. We still had fruit salad and yogurt; I like adding dry cereal to them. Ina finally woke up and wanted me to come back to bed for a Morning Prayer session!! She was on her knees praying, and I was teaching her the Lord's Prayer and the Our Father!!!

We continued on the highway, traveling in the early hours when it was not too hot. We arrived at **Alice Springs on March 15** at about noon. I made sandwiches and a salad for lunch, and we found the Alice Springs Telegraph Station Historical Reserve and toured all the buildings and attractions.

We went to a pharmacy, and I asked for some antibiotics for Ina's possible tooth infection. The lady said that she would give me what would normally be a doctor's prescription (penicillin), and I was to tell no one.

We drove west of town to the Glen Helen Gorge. It is truly a site to see with the dolomite rock cliffs. The extension to the gorge goes all the way into Alice Springs. We headed back east and stopped at the Ellery Creek Big Hole and went for a cooling-off swim; many people come here for this.

Where the Hole narrows down, the dolomite rock cliffs are beautiful, and there were some younger daredevils jumping off the cliff; I would estimate about a 40-50 foot drop. I was told the water was quite deep from some recent rains. Ina was eager to try this.

I declined, and she scooted off up the trail to do this. I asked her to get some direction when up there from the daredevils. She did a screaming jump out and down and went in feet first, the safest way she was told. She swam back to the pool. She was a competitive swimmer in her youth, and that is one thing once you learn, it never goes away.

She was very excited about the jump and wanted to do it again, but she did not like the climb to get there. She said she saw a couple of scorpions on her way up. The young crowd jumping were camped nearby, and she was invited to join them. We found their camp and set up our camper.

There were about ten of them, and the first thing I was asked was if Ina was my daughter. Ina laughed and gave me a big hug and kiss and said no, not my father; he is my lover and traveling buddy, so don't mess with me or him.

That set the tone for the behavior of the mostly young men in this group, but we had a great evening telling mostly our stories. We cooked a great supper of sausage, baked potatoes, and a salad, mostly provided from our supplies, over an open fire with cold beers. I was appreciative of Ina's initial behavior to indicate that she was not available and the group was a blast.

One of the groups had an older VW van and a flat tire. Like young people sometimes are, they came unprepared with a poor spare, so I sold them one of my spares. He did not have much money, so I took some cash and some marijuana as payment.

Ina was surprised that I smoked weed, and I was surprised that she did as well. I warned her that when I smoke weed, I usually get quite horny. Her response was to take one of the joints I had and light it up. After the effects hit, we scooted off to the van and had a very rambunctious love-making session. She really likes to pray on her knees when making love!!!

We were up early. I had not drank much and wanted to travel early when it was cool. The guy I sold the tire to was the only one up, and he commented, 'The van sure rocks.' Ina laughed; she gave me a big hug and kiss and told him how lucky she was. She told him I had pulled a tooth for her yesterday, and it still hurt but felt much better. He laughed and said in the outback, you learn to survive.

We arrived back at Alice Springs, bought a few groceries we needed, and filled up with gas. We headed north towards Darwin, thinking our next stop to be Warumungu, a five-hour travel. About one hour south of Warumungu, we looked up the Mary Ann Dam and reservoir for a swim.

A little further north, we went to the Pebbles tourist attraction. In the native language, it is called Kunjarra, and it is an important cultural site for the women of the Warunumgu tribe. The Pebbles is a sacred site. It is said the Mungar are the ancient holders of the Yawulyu song, which has spiritual powers.

We continued to Warunmungu and found a free camping site. We planned to spend the night there; the tranquility and quiet seemed spiritual. We had another joint after supper and enjoyed the effects. We were peacefully sleeping, and my spider senses woke me up.

There was a flickering of light on the pop-up screen as if a fire was burning. I never leave a fire burning, so I got up to see what was causing this. There was a small fire burning about 100 feet from our camper, and a person was sitting on a log by the fire. This caused me some concern as it was still the dead of night and we were in the middle of nowhere. It appeared to be a man, and he had heard movement from our camper, and he looked our way and waved at me to come to him.

Ina had been awakened and got up beside me and asked what was wrong. I indicated the fire and the man on the log. The man beckoned for us to come to him. I said to Ina I will go see what he wants.

I put on some shorts and got out of our camper and approached the man. He looked very old and had a friendly smile; he looked like a bushman with ragged clothes and an old hat. He said, 'My name is Jingo and I have a message for you. ' Ina had approached me from behind, and he smiled at her also.

The old man indicated that he would like us to sit on the log with him. I looked at Ina, and she whispered in my ear that he looks harmless, so let's see what he has to say.

He wanted us on either side of him, and when we were seated, he held out his hands to each of us. Ina and I took his hands, and he started to talk. He said, 'Ina and Ike, you will find your way together, and from your love and passion, you will have two children. They will have special gifts that they will not understand at a young age. Please bring them to me, and I will help them with their gifts.'

While still holding our hands, he said in his own language what I can only describe as a prayer, and let our hands go.

He got up and stirred the fire out and turned and smiled, bowing with his hands together, he bid us farewell till we returned to see him again, and he walked into the bush.

Ina and I sat there confused and were discussing this strange man and his message. How did he know our names?? We got back into the camper and resumed our sleep.

After an early light breakfast of my smoothie and coffee, we filled gas the next morning. At the gas station, we asked the owner about a strange man from the bush called Jingo. The owner told us that Jingo is a bushman, and some people think he has mystical powers. He said that he is harmless and people rarely see him.

We drove off, and the countryside had more vegetation as farther north we went. We made it to Katherine on **March 17**. It was still hot, but not like the desert for the past 4 days.

Our first stop was the Katherine Hot Springs for some soaking and relaxing. We found the Katherine Farmstay for our night camping, and the owners and staff were great. We were now in farming country, and I wanted to look up the farmer my brother Chris had worked for doing a week of fencing in 1967.

From Adelaide to Katherine, Ina has driven as much as me, which was great. When one was driving, the other one was researching our route, attractions, and possible stops when we had internet reception.

I cooked a supper of steak, rice, and a salad. Ina was enjoying the after-supper dishes and relaxing after smoking a joint. She called it our dessert!!! After dessert, we went for a tour around the farmstead; there were lots of different animals.

The next morning, I treated Ina to the Katherine Outback experience. The horse and dog trainers demonstrations were great, and much of what they did I experienced growing up on our farm back in Canada. Ina got to ride on a saddle-trained Brahma bull.

After this experience, we headed out to the Nitmiluk (Katherine) gorge. We climbed the Baruwei Lookout, which overlooks the gorge, giving a fantastic view. We had a nice swim in the gorge pool and returned to Katherine.

I had left a message for Chris's farmer friends, Jack and Mack. Jack called, and they were very pleased that I looked them up, and he gave us directions to their farm. We experienced a mid-sized beef farm and had a fantastic BBQ supper with some of his prime cuts from a steer they raised.

As it turns out, Jack is the son of the farmer my brother Chris worked for and is my age. His parents passed, and he still farms, so the discussion about Chris and his father hiring him to fence was quite interesting.

He was completely flabbergasted that I could handle a sexy package like Ina. He said I must use Viagra, but I told him no. Most of the time, I have no issue, but sometimes we just smoke a little marijuana. It worked every time, I told him.

He was curious, so I gave him a joint and suggested he smoke it about one-half hour before planned or hopeful sex and see what happens. We parked here for the night, and we had a late night telling about our journey and what my brother Chris was doing when he was here. We talked about our future traveling plans. They were great hosts.

Mack and Ina had been talking, and she said that my pulling Ina's tooth was the best solution at the time: get it out, and now let the antibiotics do their work.

We discussed with Jack and Mack the strange bushman, Jingo, who came out of the bush. We told them about his message, and Jack said he had heard of a bushman with special powers but had never seen him. Jack said, 'Do not worry about him, we have some strange men here in the bush. ' Ina and I did not dwell on the experience with the old man; it was another of those travel anomalies that just happened.

The next morning, Mack cooked up a farmer-style breakfast, and when Jack surfaced, she kissed him, and they were both smiling. Jack commented that if I could spare them, he would like a few more joints. Mack looked puzzled, and then it hit her what Jack had done. She said, 'You old bastard, I wondered what had got into you,' as we all laughed.

March 19, we set off for the last leg of our Australia route to Darwin. Jack had expressed interest in my VW van, knowing I was selling it and would think about it. He was thinking about his daughter's family; the van would make a nice fit for them. He wanted me to call him before I sold it in Darwin. He said we could maybe come to a deal, and he would come and get it. I said I wanted my money back and told him the initial cost and repairs I had completed, and it ran like a top the whole trip.

He was impressed and said he knows many people who have been stranded on a trip like we took. He would make me an offer when we were finished with it. Wow, just like that, I had a possible sale for the van!!

Darwin is a tourist destination for many; it is a big city compared to what we have experienced over the past weeks. Before reaching Darwin, we stopped and took the Spectacular Crocodile Jumping Cruise. Some of these monsters must have been twenty-five feet long and could get out of the water about ten feet going after the dangling meat.

Once in Darwin, we went to the Museum and Art Gallery of the North Territory and had supper at a fish restaurant near Nightcliff Beach. We checked in to the Knuckley Lagoon Hip camp. It had showers and a laundry facility. The washing machine was free, and we strung our clothes out on a line to dry. We had washed clothes in various swimming holes along the way and some at the Underground Hotel a few days ago.

The price of everything did not surprise us, but it is annoying after boondocking much of the way from Melbourne to Darwin.

We settled in for the night and were trying to use up the last of the marijuana joints, as we would not want any drugs when traveling to Timor-Leste.

Ina was laughing when she recalled Jack wanting some joints to try and see if it helped make him horny.

Ina was apprehensive about the next leg of our journey. She had been researching Timor-Leste and advised that the prices are not good for most everything and that we would miss the amenities and convenience of the van. We enjoyed the van's bed again after smoking a joint and were savoring our time in the van, as we had been in it nearly a month.

We woke and were trying to use up the last of our food, so we had a smoothie, boiled eggs, and yogurt.

We backtracked a bit and traveled about forty minutes to the Florence Falls Water hole. It was as nice as many of the water holes we had used, and we went for a swim in the crystal clear water.

A little ways back towards Darwin, we stopped at Tolmer Falls and lay in the sun for a few hours, then swam in its water hole as well. It was nice not to think of traveling longer distances.

On the way back to Darwin, we found a boondocking location and set up camp for the night. We built a little fire, cooked our last potatoes and steak on an open fire, and enjoyed the quiet, but the mosquitoes were buzzing. We smoked our second last joint and set the van rocking as usual.

In the morning, we had more of our dry cereal with kiwi and yogurt from our supplies. We were whittling our food down to the very little left. Going back to Darwin, we stopped at a used car lot; I was curious about the value of the van here in Darwin.

A typical salesman was yapping away about this and that which was wrong with the van, and after a half hour of this, Ina surprised me and asked him to put up an offer or shut up. He looked at her and laughed, saying she was one tough lady. He offered us 5000.

I showed him my receipts for the repairs in Sydney, and I smiled and said to Ina, let's go. He was increasing his offer as we were sitting in the van, and I said, double your first offer, and I would think about it. He did not want us to leave and went to see his boss; he came back and suggested their best offer was $8500. I started the van and handed him my phone number, telling him that he had my price.

We went to the Darwin airport and spent hours checking the prices of flights from Darwin to Oecussi or Dilli on Timor-Leste Island. The price was about $250 US dollars.

Then flights from Dilli or Oecussi to Manila in the Philippines, where I planned to travel to after Timor-Leste, were between 250 and 600. A flight from Darwin to Manila was only $600.

We were debating whether to even stop in Timor-Leste or travel directly to Manila in the Philippines. My destination in the Philippines was my friends Barry and Liberty's house, which they had built there in 2025. We could stay there for a period of time that we needed to tour the Philippines and then carry on from there. We knew that travel and accommodations after this would be more costly than our trip to this point.

We scooted back out to the boondocking site from last night, built a fire, and cooked almost the last of our food. It was wearing on both of us the uncertainty of all our travel arrangements after this. We felt so comfortable in the van.

We smoked our last joint, and the van was rocking one more time. We slept like logs and were very sorry to get up, it was possibly our last night in the van. In the morning, we finished the last of our breakfast food and packed what little we had left in our little cooler.

I called Jack with our plans to possibly leave Darwin in the next day or so. He was willing to match my request to recover the money I had in the van, which was $5000. I did not tell him we could get more, but a "deal is a deal"; I was standing by my word. Ina was quite pleased that I did this; she said I was true to my word, and in today's world, that is unusual.

Jack would arrive later in the day, and we would complete the deal. We were both feeling sorry to see the van go.

On March 22, we booked at the Mercure Darwin Airport Resort, which was within walking distance from the terminal. We finished the last of our food and cleaned the van out as well as we could

We took it to a car wash and sprayed it down; we stripped the bed and were all ready for Jack and Mack. They arrived at 1 pm and were quite happy to get the van for his daughter's family.

Ina told them we would dearly miss it, as we had spent a month traveling in it with so many memories and experiences from Sydney to Darwin.

I had wanted half in cash and the rest with an e-transfer. We settled all the paperwork. I told Mack to wash the bedding, and they were on their way. Jack drove the van, and Mack drove their car. We waved goodbye, and Ina was crying; she said, 'I love that van.'

We settled into our room and then went to the swimming pool and hot tub. We were living in luxury now compared to our last month. We had a delicious pasta supper at the resort restaurant, and Ina called her parents with an update on our travel progress.

Her mother was very concerned about traveling to Timor-Leste and suggested we go directly to the Philippines as that plan sounded much safer. We talked about the pros and cons of going to Timor-Leste.

I was interested to see the people; it would not be the same as my brothers Les and Chris had experienced, and we would not be walking. The political upheaval and government had settled out over the last ten years, but still, rebels, thieves, and thugs lived in the backwoods and in poor sections of the towns and villages.

The possibility of violence against us, I thought, would be minimal as we would stay in safe areas, but one never knows. I took into account the fact that Ina was a very obvious target because of her beauty, and they would consider her wealthy.

We debated where we would travel and how. It would have to be on the main road from Oescussi to Dili or vice-versa to be safe with Ina with me. So what would we see and do? We would be limited and often in danger. We decided on Manila in the Philippines.

March 24, we booked to Manila in the Philippines. We left Darwin at 20:50 and had a stop in Bali, then on to Manila, arriving at 6 pm on March 24. We had to purchase visas and check through customs with no issue, except totally unpacking my backpack. We chose a cheaper hotel, the Privato Hotel Makati, for $38/night.

I contacted Barry and Liberty about a week ago about the possibility of our coming to their home to visit, whether they were there or not. I had not heard back from them, so now, in Manila, I was attempting to reach them again. I left a message like I had before, but maybe I missed a call or text with poor cell reception.

Ina wanted to have a swim and then maybe go out for a drink. We were not hungry after finishing all our food from the van, so we had a swim and shower. Showers Ina prefers with a naked man; she goes crazy with the soap, keeps dropping it, and just loves it. We went for one drink and went back to our room.

Chapter 4
"Aussie to the Philippines"

We were lying in bed, and Barry called us from their house. They had arrived two days ago and were surprised where we were and they would be delighted and would arrange to come get us or find us a ride the next day. He asked me when you say we, what exactly does that mean when I told him, he said, ya right, don't bullshit me.

On March 26, Barry and Liberty came to pick us up themselves. Barry is thunderstruck by Ina; she is a bombshell and affects many men the same; they are speechless. Barry, being Barry, said to her, 'What the hell are you doing with this old man?' She was laughing and said, 'Just going with the flow, and we both like sex a lot.' She stirs the deep gut feeling in most men. Liberty gave Ina a hug and told her she was with a good old man. Ina laughed at that and told her she was lucky.

The ride around the Talim Lake to their house in the Paagahan Laguna area takes about 3 hours. They had the house built in 2024/25, and it is beautiful.

Ina and I had our own bedroom, and they even had a swimming pool. I had a lot of questions about the house, and Barry had plans for me to help him with some landscaping for my rent!!

Liberty had the kitchen all organized and planned a great Filipino supper of roast pig and all the trimmings. We had a great night with lots of drinking after supper, and the tales everyone was telling were lively conversations. Ina told the tooth story and showed them the hole. Barry said, 'That is nothing for Ike to do; he is a Jack of all trades.'

Like old times, Barry and I got into the sauce too much, and I tired out about midnight. The jet lag was not bad, but still, travel for my age is always difficult. Ina and Liberty chatted much longer as they got along like a house on fire.

We had a Filipino breakfast of bangus, Pandesal, Champorado, Kakanin, and Torta. It helped the hangover. We had a good hot coffee to follow, and Ina took hers to the pool as her bikini was under the house coat Liberty had provided her with. Barry was all eyes as she took off her housecoat, and Liberty gave him a look.

After chatting for a couple of hours, Liberty had plans for her and Ina to go shopping. Ina had expressed that she does like shopping but had very little time for it on our trip and found out that I do not like it at all.

Barry got me saddled into some manual labor on some landscaping with cold beer breaks as required.

Ina and Liberty arrived back with many bags full. She had a great time and said everything was so cheap. They planned more of these trips.

Liberty is all about family, and some of her family were coming over that night to meet us, and we had another feast. Ina was busy with Liberty for hours preparing all the food. She really enjoyed Liberty's company. She said she was like a soul mate, and they just met.

Liberty's family is a jovial bunch, full of questions about my and Ina's travels. They were very surprised at my age and especially Ina's age when thinking of us together.

In a crowd, Ina is a little shy, but as the night passes and a little wine, she loosens up, and her laughter is infectious. It was a little cool as night set in, and we had a fire pit going beside the pool. I had asked Barry about snakes, and they like the heat from fires, but he had not seen many yet.

Everyone left about midnight and was saying see you on the weekend, as apparently something was planned and the crowd would be much larger.

"Aussie to the Philippines"

For the next two days, Liberty and Ina disappeared for half a day or more. Barry kept the whip going with our landscaping work, and we were getting lots done.

The girls had a feast planned for the weekend, as Liberty expected about fifty people. A couple of her cousins played guitars, so a Filipino sing-song was planned. Ina was enthralled with all these preparations and was up to her elbows helping Liberty.

Liberty told me she is a ball of fire, always thinking and working really hard. I said to Liberty, because we talk about sex some, 'You should see her in bed.' Liberty had a real gut laugh at that.

After supper that night, Ina told me she overheard me and Liberty talking about sex, and she was a little upset and embarrassed. I said Liberty and I talk like that sometimes, as neither of us is shy. She was ok with that but did not want me talking about her to people this weekend like that. I assured her I was not a braggart or the type of person to embarrass her. She said she knew that because in our time together, she never heard anything from me like that. We were having more or less our first serious or difficult chat, and she crawled on top of me and showed me more of the passion and energy she always has.

The weekend was a great time. All the people that came brought food. We had a spread that made your chops water just by looking at it. Liberty's cousin was great with a computer and downloaded our phone-stored photos of my and Ina's pictures from our trip. We watched a photo show that Ina and I narrated. There were many questions about how I managed with the three girls; Ina assured them I was hers only.

Only one couple had been to New Zealand and Australia, but not a trip like that through the outback. Ina showed her prized opal, and one of Liberty's cousins, who was a jeweler, offered to cut it and make two rings. He and Ina made a deal to complete this and chose the kind of rings, and she provided a shipping address for him to send the rings when completed. She paid him the full fee as she trusted Liberty's cousin. It is amazing how little things like that make a trip so memorable.

Ina was walking around with a video call to her parents in Sweden, showing them everything and the celebration we were having, and they told her we made the right choice to skip Indonesia. Her mother told her she may have made the right choice to travel with Ike.

It was a very late night or early morning when most of the guests had left. There were a few that were curled up fast asleep or passed out. There was a drink that was passed around called

'**Lambanog,**' a distilled coconut drink of about 40% alcohol, which is deadly. It comes in many flavors, but the mango and pineapple flavors that were brought were so easy to drink but hit hard after too many. Many of the guests wanted to cheer me and Ina, so by the end of the evening, we were both pretty sloshed.

Barry and Liberty were so happy they had this gathering, as they had not had a party at their new house. It was a superb success. It must have been; my head hurt all day.

Barry and Liberty did not have a car yet, so I rented an SUV, and we planned some touring. Since Liberty was born and raised here, she knows many places and things to see and do.

On **March 30,** we set off traveling north with plans to see the Batad Rice Terraces. We visited Cale Crisologo, where the architecture is very old, and there are many horse taxis.

Our first night, we stayed in the Pagudpud area in the Palm Grove Saud Holiday Complex. It was right on the ocean, and a bargain at $58/room and food was great. We all went for a dip in the ocean; the waves crashing in were huge. The drive all the way is along the ocean at times, and the scenery is spectacular.

After a traditional breakfast of rice cake, spicy meat, and greens with strong coffee, we were off to continue our tour, going around the north end of the island and then heading back south.

Many places are great for landscape photos from various viewpoints, but the best is at the Claveria view deck. We crossed the Magapit suspension bridge, the oldest bridge in the Philippines, and toured the Castle in the Sky near the bridge. Our next stop was the Callao Cave, with its historic history.

We stopped in Cauayan City, toured Our Lady of the Pillar church, and stayed at the Family Farm Stay, with the family running it, and we had authentic dishes with breakfast included at $69/night.

We continued south along the coast and in the mountains. The flora everywhere is so lush and of such a variety. We walked the Baler Hanging Bridge near Suclavin. It was pretty old and rusted, and the concrete supports on each end were showing their age. We made it back on **April 2** to Barry and Liberty's house and relaxed in the pool.

We relaxed the next day around the pool, sipping beers and discussing our trip. Liberty advised that her brother, who has the original family home, had invited us there for supper and an evening of visiting.

We had more traditional dishes, which always included rice and spicy meats. There was more **'Lambanog,'** but we were only sipping it carefully this night. Ina and I had a few nights with no sex, just nice cuddling and sleep, so this night brought a renewed Ina-style activity with much enthusiasm.

During the day, we were discussing with Barry and Liberty. A trip going south with some ferry island hopping to the very south island in the area of Soccsksargen to General Santos City. The city has a rich and sad history with the original B'laan nomadic people's first inhabitants, who were eventually pushed out into the surrounding hills, not unlike other tribes in these islands.

The night before, Ina and I had discussed that we would like to continue our planned trip on my brother's route. We planned on flying to Singapore and traveling north through Malaysia, Thailand, Burma, and India, with a final stop in Nepal. Our final stop in Nepal included a 2-3 week stay at a yoga and meditation retreat in the Himalayan Mountains.

Since the duration of our travels for the rest of this planned route was not set, Ina had to go back to work from her leave of absence. Her plans for about 3 month's maximum duration on this trip would expire in Nepal. She said never in her wildest dreams would she have envisioned how her trip would extend beyond her plans for New Zealand and Australia.

We were not sure of plans after the yoga and meditation retreat; one possibility was flying to Sweden and spending some time meeting her parents.

I was very troubled by these thoughts because, at some point, I must have serious discussions with Ina about our future. Why an old man like me would not want to spend the rest of my life with a fantastic woman like Ina?

We had never discussed a family. Would I ever consider being a father again at 75??? These things were running through my mind; I was considering Ina's life much more than mine. We had become quite attached to each other. We tolerated each other, we laughed a lot, we were respectful of each other, we had great sex, and we had many of the same likes and dislikes.

But she was only 32, less than half my age, and had so much of her life to live. Would she want to be saddled with a guy over the hill and on the way down from here???

We discussed our plans to move on with our planned route to India and Nepal. Barry and Liberty had lots to do to complete their house and landscaping plans, so they were sad about our plans to leave but understood our plans. We booked flights to Singapore the next day, **April 5.** Our plans were to ride trains or buses north through Malaysia, Thailand, Burma, and India.

That night, we had our final supper at Barry and Liberty, and it was a happy affair. Liberty and Ina had a bang-up meal again. We relaxed around the pool, and Ina had to package up most of her purchases from the shopping trips with Liberty to ship to her parents in Sweden. It was mostly clothing which is light. She and Liberty scooted off for one last short shopping trip, and they posted her large box as well.

That night, lying in bed, Ina was quiet and sad; she expressed her fondness for Liberty and Barry from our stay here. She said friends like them are hard to find and must be cherished. She thought, at some point, we would return to make the island hopping trip south.

I never commented on this statement, as I was flashing ahead about my thoughts about our future. I knew, at some point, we must address this, and maybe the next month of travel would bring these thoughts and discussions to some resolution for us. Ina was looking in my eyes and suggested I had something on my mind, and I kissed her, but the monthly moon time was on, damn.

Chapter 5
"Singapore and Malaysia"

We were all packed and had an early breakfast as our flight was mid-morning. At the departure area, we said our goodbyes, and Ina and Liberty had tears in their eyes. Our flight departed on time, and the flight to Singapore was four hours. We arrived in Singapore on time **on April 6.**

I did not look forward to visiting Singapore; it is a small country but essentially one large city with a population of nearly six million, making it one of the most densely populated countries in the world. Since we were so near, it made sense to visit it, but for only one day. Ina agreed and she was as interested as me, but of the same frame of mind that it is just another big damn city.

Singapore is only 712 square kilometers with a population of almost 6 million people, so every square foot is used up. It is surrounded by an inlet between it and Malaysia. Originally a British colony, it obtained independence in 1959, joined Malaysia in 1963, and seceded from Malaysia in 1963. It is known as a global financial center, and it is one of the busiest ports in the world.

Ina had researched Singapore because of her background in economics and her employment in investments. She had considered trying to move there to live, but the cost of living was one of the highest in the world. She was happy to live in her home in Sweden, but spoke of the riches to be made in the financial world of business and investments in Singapore, if one is willing to take the risk of the high cost of living. Her company only deals with some companies based in Singapore, but has never had plans to open an office there.

We researched all the things to see here, as it is also a great tourist attraction. Singapore is known to be a safe country that attracts tourists who like big city action that is also safe. We booked a cheap room at the Classique Hotel and went on a walking tour of downtown, which seemed to be everywhere!! We booked a Lion City Bike tour the next day. We immediately looked to book train transportation north to Kuala Lumpur, the capital of Malaysia, for the following day.

The nightlife on our first night was very lively, people were everywhere, as many as a honey bee hive, and a cosmopolitan blend. We had a fish supper and enjoyed a couple of drinks at a pub. Our room was fine, and we found a nice restaurant for breakfast—everything was expensive.

Our bike tour included the Marina Bay, the Singapore River, Merlion Park, Telok Ayer market, Chinatown, Little India, Haji Lane and the Kampong Glam neighbourhood. It is a clean and organized city, but we both felt overwhelmed by the crowds, city smells, and congestion everywhere.

We were mostly on the east end of the city, but we had no desire to see the rest. We went for a Hainanese chicken rice, chilli crab, and Laksa supper, and bought our train tickets to Kuala Lumpur for the next day. We chose to travel as far as Gemas overnight, a town 4 hours north of Singapore. We had an early night, Ina was tired, and I had a night off!!

April 8, we took a cab to the railway station, the cabbie attempted to overcharge us, they are super expensive, bastards. We had to go through customs and buy a visa for Malaysia. The train was not a bullet train, but it was fast. The scenery was great and the seats were comfortable. We arrived about 2 pm and looked up a hotel that the train porter knew, his wife ran it, the Azhar Avocado.

We took a cab to the Gemas paddy rice fields and had a nice tour of the operation of a rice paddy farm.

"Singapore and Malaysia"

We had supper out at the farm, Azhar Avocado, the porter's wife cooked a traditional Malaysian supper of Nas lemak, coconut rice and spicy sambal (a spicy sauce), and Rendang, a rich coconut stew (cooked with lemongrass, galangal, garlic, turmeric, ginger, Shallots and chillies). We had the traditional teh tarik, a strong black tea poured back and forth with condensed milk, which creates a head (froth).

Back in our room, I had brought a bottle of Lao-Lao rice whiskey, and we had a couple of shooters of that with more tea. Our room was comfortable, more like we were at a home than a hotel. Ina was at the moon time of the month, so there was no sex, at least not for her, and she can handle a microphone very well!!!

The train ride to Kuala Lumpur left early, and we arrived around noon on **April 9**. We took a cab to the Homestay Villa Hotel Mas Guest House. The owner operator, Omar, was a great guy, the place was clean, but I always check for bed mites and cockroaches. He offered to cook a traditional supper of BBQ chicken. He suggested some attractions to see, and he would rent us his car. I declined the car rental and we took a cab to the Thean Hou Tempal, the Petronas Twin Towers, and the National Zoo of Malaysia.

We arrived back at the Homestay, Omar BBQed a great supper with the curried rice, and the chicken had a tangy sauce. He served the tea tarik, and I brought our Lao-Lao rice whiskey. Omar suggested we take a train, or at least part of the way, as buses were not great and the roads were busy.

We decided on the train from Kuala Lumpur to George Town, which cost about $50 each. For a three-and-a-half-hour ride, that was quite cheap. Omar would give us a lift to the train station the next day.

Thanks to Omar, we had a nice breakfast and a lunch to go, and we arrived in time for our train and relaxed in comfort. The seats are much like an aircraft seat and recline very nicely. The scenery is great, and I had a book to read.

Ina loved to lie on my shoulder or lap and sleep; she said the train motion made her sleepy. She curls up like a dog and snoozes away. The train passed through Penang, and we arrived at Butterworth on **April 10**.

Then you take a cab or ferry across to Georgetown, which is on an island. We took a cab to the Flamingo Hotel by the Beach, a little more upscale than some we had stayed at. Ina was having some menstrual cramps and needed to relax.

After some relaxing, we went to the pool and relaxed some more. Ina was feeling better, so we took a cab to the Penang Trishaw Station and took a one-hour ride around Georgetown with multiple stops for shopping and photos. One stop, as the Leony San Teng Khoo Kongsi (a local historical museum) and Tariz, our driver was only too happy to wait, even though it overran our one hour.

Many of the cab or Trishaw drivers have friends they network with to bring in customers. Tariz, our trishaw driver, asked us if we wanted to go to his friend's restaurant. We agreed where we had the appetizer which was Pholes, a snack made with a batter from flour, eggs, sugar, coconut, milk and yeast cooked in a fish oil, then the main dish was, Penang famous Laksa, a rice noodle dish with sardine broth, condiments and seasoning followed by the tea tarik.

I was a little surprised that our driver asked if he could join us for dinner. I was sure he thought Ina was my daughter, and he was completely enthralled with her. She did not mind the attention, but when he asked her if he could take her dancing if her father did not mind, Ina laughed really hard, got up, sat on my lap, and gave me a big kiss. The owner was laughing so much because he and our driver had been talking in their own language, and he knew the driver was smitten or for sure very interested in her.

I got a spidery feeling about these two, not a good feeling because there are so many scam artists in the orient. They seemed to discuss a lot about me and Ina. He got a free meal and then gave us a free ride back to our hotel.

He offered to sell us some marijuana joints, we had not had any since Australia, and so we bought only one. We had a nice swim and were checking train schedules for the next day. We smoked the joint on the balcony and enjoyed the effects.

I called my nephew in Mumbai, India, to get his ex-wife's phone number in Thailand. He had some idea I was taking a trip, but was not aware of the details. When I described my trip so far and my travelling companions and then single companion, he said 'Uncle don't bullshit me,' same thing my friend Barry had said. He wondered why I should stop and see his ex-wife. I told him why not, I was here.

When he realized I would be in Hat Yai the next day, he was flabbergasted, still not believing how I was travelling. I said I would call him back on a video call and he was blithering like he thought I was nuts and was setting him up with a fake Ina, who he thought was just a hooker in Thailand.

I told him, Ina and I would see him in Mumbai. He gave me Su's number and still did not believe Ina and I were travelling together. Ina was laughing and confused about why he did not believe me. I told her a tiny bit about Mike's and my time in Thailand, and I think she got the picture.

It did not surprise me that Tariz, the trishaw driver, was waiting at our hotel lobby. He could not wait to see Ina again, but it was too far for him to take us across the channel to Butterworth train station. He looked like a dog that had lost his bone. But he was resourceful and asked where we were going, and we told him Hat Yai in the district of Songkhla, Thailand.

He offered a service that his friend does with a minivan for about RM 35 ($11). We thought a change to road travel in a nice air-conditioned minivan would be a nice change. Tariz was on his phone yammering away with his friend, and we grabbed a cab over to Butterworth train station and met the minivan there. Tariz was storing our bags in the trishaw carrier and spending extra time doing this.

Chapter 6
"Thai Minefields and Scoundrels"

It was longer than a train ride, and the driver had a few planned stops, some to drop people, the border crossing, and his favorite restaurant, which his friend has in Thailand. The mini-bus was not crowded and we had a triple seat to ourselves, which allowed Ina and me to stretch out on each other's laps.

The border crossing seemed to go quite smoothly, no visa required, and luggage was not checked. A dog did a walk-through the mini-van and he stood on his hind legs to smell the luggage. He spent more time near my bag than I liked. I thought he might smell the marijuana smoke lingering on the clothes I had in my bag from last night. His handler gave me a funny look and pulled the dog away. This puzzled me.

We arrived in **Hat Yai** on **April 12** at the train terminal in mid-afternoon. Mike must have called Su, because she knew I was coming and was overjoyed that I thought of her, and I could come right over to her house. She said Mike thinks I was bullshitting him about a travel companion.

I told her Ina and I would see her in about one hour. We took a taxi from Hat Yai north to the town of Meikri, where Su lives. She gave me a big hug and was chatting away, so glad I remembered her and stopped to visit. She hugged Ina and asked how she liked Thailand.

I had not seen Su for about 10 years, and she looked much the same, like she had not aged one bit. She had a supper planned and showed us her house and where we would sleep.

I told her we booked a room at the resort I stayed at the last time I was here. She was disappointed we would not stay; she would make room for us here, but I declined. We talked about Ford, her son, who was now in university in Bangkok. I asked her how her English teaching business is going, and she said it pays the bills.

She was very curious about me and Ina. Ina told her she is very happy travelling with me, she said I am a good man, and she is safe with me. We told her about how we met in New Zealand, travelled with the two English girls, then split up in Sydney, Australia, and just the two of us travelled through Australia and then into the Philippines, Singapore, and Malaysia.

We told her our plans to go to Chang Mi to visit Garret, my brother's old friend, and continue to New Delhi, India, and on to Kathmandu in Nepal for a yoga and meditation retreat. I told her about my brother Les's trip, and she was blown away by my trying to retrace Les's trip.

I sent an e-mail to Garret in Chang Mi. I told him where I was and if he would have us for a visit in a few days. He was hesitant; I think he did not believe me, from his response. I asked for his phone number and sent a photo from Su's place. He then said to call him when we arrived at Chang Mi airport.

Su, Ina, and I chatted for hours, and she started to cook supper, which included BBQ chicken and fried rice with veggies mixed in. We enjoyed our conversation and meal immensely; she was such an inquisitive and humble lady.

We told her we had booked flights from Hat Yi to Chang Mi the next day. It was late, and she gave us a ride to the resort about one mile away. She wanted to have us over for breakfast in the morning and take us to the airport. She said that we are at a crossroads in our lives and we should address it.

When we were back at the resort, Ina and I were discussing what Su meant with her comment about a crossroads. I told her I was not sure, but that we needed to talk about us. We talked about our plans and the time limit for Ina to return to Sweden and resume her job and career. Our new plan was to fly to Chiang Mai and visit Garret, then fly to New Delhi and Kathmandu to go on the yoga and meditation retreat. This plan would take about one month, and Ina would have to fly back to Sweden.

Ina was very sad, and she said she was thinking about what our plans together were. She was holding and kissing me like she would never let go, and we fell into bed with a desperation in our lovemaking. When we were spent and exhausted, we were lying in bed entwined together, and Ina was crying. She said, 'What are we going to do? I do not want to leave you.'

I told her I am in love with her and I feel like her, that I do not want to leave her. She was crying with tears of joy, and she said, 'She loves me also, and after Nepal, would I come to Sweden with her?' I told her we both need to think about this over the next month and make the best path forward to suit both of us. She thought I was not committing to her, and I should be honest with her.

I asked her what her plans were for a family. She said, 'I want a child with you, I want us to be a family.' I asked her if she considered my age and how long I would be alive. She said that does not matter, she knows I would be a great father, and when I age and die, she will have experienced what she wants, it would be difficult to deal with, but our child would be old enough to handle it, and she would have to manage. I explained that it is possible but difficult to have a child with my input because of my tubes being tied.

I kissed her and said, 'Let's sleep on it, and take it one day at a time, and be open about our plans and talk about it whenever it comes up.' We both agreed that we had left it this long, but our travel had been a busy time, and it seemed never the right time to discuss this topic. We fell asleep with I think both of us somewhat satisfied we had approached the necessary topics and had a path forward we both agreed to.

We woke up, showered, and Ina pulled me back in bed, and we made love with an urgency like there was no tomorrow. We walked to Su's place and talked the whole way about our future. Ina was convinced we would be together forever. I did not tell her, but I was not so sure.

Su, I think, sensed something important had happened between Ina and me, and she asked if I was going to leave Ina after Nepal. I explained that both Ina and I had very short talks about this on our journey so far about what our long-range plans were, but there was never the right time and place. I told her last night that we discussed this topic at great length, and were committed to each other, and I would likely travel to Sweden with Ina when we completed our trip in Nepal.

After a hearty breakfast, Su gave us a ride to the airport in Hat Yi. She said Ina and I looked different from yesterday, and thought we should talk about our future whenever the topic came up. She was a sensitive lady and read our thoughts with telepathic abilities. We had a tri hug, and Ina was crying, thanking her for her thoughts.

Ina told Su she thought she had triggered our night of addressing this topic, and that she was a very smart and thoughtful lady. Su wished us the best and invited us back anytime we are travelling this way.

Our flight was 4 hours and cost $58 each. On **April 14,** we arrived in Chang Mi. When we went to collect our luggage, there were numerous policemen standing with a dog sitting right beside my bag. The police stopped me when I went to pick up my bag and asked me to identify myself and if that was my bag. I immediately flashed back to the dog sniffing our bags at the border crossing from Malaysia to Thailand. The dog had spent more time sniffing my and Ina's bags, and I thought maybe he was getting a lingering odour from our clothes from the night before that we had on when smoking the joint.

I was now worried because a dope dog sat beside a bag that may have dope in it. I had no choice but to unpack my bag, and much to my surprise and dismay, stuffed near the bottom under some clothes, there was a bag of marijuana in it; I would say about two to three ounces.

They asked me again if this was my bag, and I said yes, and this is not my dope. Someone must have put it there? Ina was observing all this and was trying to talk with them, saying the same things as I. They asked her for identification, if we were together, and if she had a bag also. She said yes and had her bag beside her. They asked her to unpack her bag and found no drugs in it.

They read me my rights, took all my possessions and marijuana, cuffed me, and advised that I was being charged with possession of an illegal drug in Thailand and would be held for this possible offence, and I could consult a lawyer.

I was beyond worried and scared shitless. We had not purchased the marijuana, and my thoughts immediately went to the trishaw driver Tariz and his attention to Ina and me in Georgetown. I was assuming he had planted the marijuana and likely thought we would get caught at the border.

My thoughts were extremely desperate, what would happen to me, and what about Ina? I asked if I could talk to Ina, and I told her to get a hotel room, and we will get through this.

She was crying and extremely upset, but this did not matter to the police. I said what I thought about Tariz from Georgetown and that he was collaborating with the restaurant owner and the van driver in preying on people like us, especially a beautiful blonde like her. She said, 'What do you mean? I said, 'How enthralled he was with her and would do anything to get her in his control somehow.' She said, I will protect myself, and I will make these police see this.

We had little choice, and they took me away. As we were leaving the luggage area, I noticed a man watching us. He had a hoodie on and sunglasses, and he looked familiar. At the police station, I was officially charged with being in Thailand with an illegal substance and would be held in custody until my court appearance.

Anyone's worst fears were happening to me, and I flashed back to thoughts that this trip was too good to be true. The police spent hours questioning me about my travel history, my future travel plans, my relationship with Ina, and anything they could think of to make me worry and tell them something that I had no clue about what they wanted to hear.

Finally, after a few hours, they asked if I would like to make a phone call. I said yes, and they took me to a little room, which I am sure was bugged, and I asked for my phone, and I called Garret.

He came down to the police station, and he was allowed to see me; he professed to be my lawyer. We greeted each other, and we both thought the same thing: how could this happen?

He first asked what the charges were and how I came into possession of the marijuana. I told him the whole story, including my suspicion of the trishaw driver Tariz, the restaurant owner, and the van driver. He asked where Ina is, and I told him what I advised her to do and gave him her phone number and e-mail. I asked him to contact her and to please go see her and look after her. I told him about seeing a man at the airport watching us when the police were arresting me, and he looked familiar. He assured me he would immediately contact her.

Garret left, and I was put in a holding cell, the first ever in my life, and I was sick to my stomach. My trip had taken an unexpected turn with dire consequences, I assumed.

I knew Garret from my experiences in Edmonton in 1973; he was a very get-r-dun kind of guy. He had said I will find the bastard, and he will confess and then pay. I had seen what Garret could do with his fists and feet. He was older now, but when emailing back and forth, he had told me he had taken up Jujitsu here and was in great shape. What could I do but wait???

Ina had left the airport and booked into a hotel nearby. She was understandably upset beyond words and called the Canadian consulate and explained her situation. They would look into it, and she should come there to file a report. She called the Swedish consulate and explained her situation again and was advised to come and file a report.

She then called her father in Sweden and explained the situation to him. Her father is a criminal lawyer, and after much discussion, he told her to sit tight and he would fly to Chang Mi and help her out. She explained to him that she was not in any trouble, but I was. He understood this and asked her to be calm and safe till he arrived, and he would handle the matter once in Thailand.

She went to the restaurant in the hotel and ordered a meal. As she was sitting there, she noticed a man watching her, and she was terrified to recognize the trishaw driver Tariz. He smiled at her and approached her table. She was so scared that she was frozen in her chair.

He explained that he had business here, and it was such a coincidence that he met her here. She knew right away that he was the perpetrator of this sordid situation. She knew that he would try to chat with her and, in some way, try to help her out, but it would only be a ploy to convince her of his well-meaning intention; he had other ulterior motives; she was terrified of his real intentions.

He proceeded to chat with her and asked where I was. She did not want to alert him that I was detained by the police, but thought the bastard might already know that. She told him I was arranging a car rental and would return soon. She thought he must have followed them to Chang Mi after we were not detained by the Thai border patrol when we crossed from Malaysia. Her mind was churning with what to do. She was scared but extremely angry; maybe a good combination with what was going through her mind.

Right then, she got a text and said she had to answer this and said that it was me, and I would be about one hour. It was actually from Garret, and he asked where she was. She sent back her hotel name and room number, and said that she was in trouble. He said to sit tight in a public place, and he would come right away. She shut her phone off and was thinking of alerting the police.

Tariz could not do anything with her in the restaurant, but was trying to act calm and convince her that he would help her in any way he could. She was trying to tell him that she did not need any help, or especially his help, and he could go about his business. She needed the washroom and went to use it. When she returned, Tariz was still there.

She was also thirsty from this threat sitting in front of her, and drank some of her water. She thought it tasted a little off, but lots of water in our travels tasted off.

After a couple of minutes, she felt a little drowsy, and Tariz was quickly beside her and helped her to her feet. He spoke Hindi and explained to the waiter he was helping her out because she was feeling drowsy.

He helped her from the restaurant through the lobby and took the elevator up to her room, holding her up with his arm under hers and walking her along. In the room, he lay her down on the bed, closed and locked the door.

When Garret left the police, he was not far from the hotel, and he drove there to find Ina. He entered the lobby and checked the restaurant. He asked about a blond lady. The waiter told him that she was not feeling well, and her boyfriend said he was helping her to her room. He checked with the front desk, and they advised him that she and her boyfriend had taken the elevator as she was not feeling well and were going to her room.

Garret decided he likely needed a key to get in, and he lied that he was her father and needed to go see her to find out what was wrong. They reluctantly agreed after much discussion, when he explained that he was from here. He showed his Thai identification and said he wanted to surprise her, but did not realize she was not feeling well.

They said it was only minutes ago that they had gone to her room. They gave him a card, and he took the elevator up to the floor of her room and proceeded to her room. He was not sure what to expect, but he thought the best plan would be to surprise the guy who was accompanying her. Garret used the card to unlock the door and burst in.

He immediately saw a woman on the bed, not moving. He assumed it was Ina lying on the bed, obviously not awake, and this obviously non-native Thai guy to this country with his skin color, sitting beside her, talking on his cell phone.

The guy jumped up and started yelling in Hindi at Garret. Garret is a get-r-dun kind of guy, and he was across the room and kicked the guy in the head. He went down like a sack of potatoes.

He checked Ina, who was pleasantly sleeping, but her vital signs seemed ok. Garret took a lamp cord, ripped the cord out of the lamp, and tied the guy's hands behind his back. He took off his one boot and sock and stuffed the sock in the guy's mouth.

Garret checked on Ina, who was moaning and appeared to be coming awake. He had some time on his hands as the guy was still unconscious.

Ina was slowly coming awake, and she was completely confused and terrified to see a stranger in the room. When she saw Tariz on the floor with his hand bound and a sock in his mouth, she seemed to relax.

She took at least ten minutes to recover enough to ask who Garret was, and he told her and asked her to remain calm as he had things to do. He asked what happened, and she explained that this guy is Tariz from Georgetown and had approached her at the restaurant table and was trying to convince her he had only run into her by coincidence and would help her. She was very scared and she went to the washroom, came back, and he was still there talking to her, and she drank some of her water.

Garret pondered this for a minute and asked her to remain calm and, if he regained consciousness, to just keep away from him or leave the room. She said she had a brown belt in jujitsu and would be fine.

Garret left the room and returned to the hotel restaurant. He went to the waiter and asked which table the blonde lady sat at. She showed him, and he asked her if this was her water. She told him it was her glass, and he took it. He said she needed water.

He returned to Ina's room, and Tariz was sitting up and very angry, but when he saw Garret, his attitude changed to fear.

Ina was standing in front of him, and he was looking at her with glaring eyes. She looked at Garret and turned and kicked Tariz on the chin with her right foot. He slumped to the floor. Ina was considering more punishment, but Garret said we can do that later, right now we need him talking, and we will video everything he says. He will tell us what we want, or he will suffer.

Ina did not know Garrett's background and the kind of punishment he could and would inflict if needed. After a few minutes and a cold glass of water in his face, Tariz came to and looked quite scared.

Garret explained what they needed and what would happen if he refused to cooperate. Garret explained that he lived here, and he had police friends who would help if required, and if he did not cooperate, he would just end up floating down the river.

They gave him some time, and Garret approached him and was squeezing specific nerves in the back of Tariz's neck, which caused considerable pain. Tariz was moaning and twitching. Garret informed him that he would remove the sock from his mouth, but if he tried yelling, he would get much more of the pain.

He gave him a little time, inflicted some more pain, and asked if he was ready to answer questions. He nodded his agreement, and Garret removed the sock from his mouth.

Tariz did not know he was being recorded. After a few serious cuffs to the head and more excruciating neck pain, Tariz told the story they needed to hear about planting the marijuana in my bag and thought they would be detained at the border, but the dog missed it, and he had to follow them to Chang Mi.

Garret got details, including what Tariz had put in Ina's water, which he had a sample of. Tariz did not know this. Garret conferred with Ina if she had anything she wanted to know. She said she wanted to know what he was going to do with her.

Tariz would not tell them that even with multiple cuffs to his noggin and neck pain from Garret. Ina was so relieved; she gave Garret a hug and thanked him for his help. Garret called his wife and explained nothing, only that he would be late.

Garret did have friends with the police, and he was on his phone with them. They advised him to sit tight, and they would be there very soon.

They arrived in about fifteen minutes, and Garret explained the situation. They thought there may not be enough evidence, even with two people's stories, both white people.

Garret explained about the water and showed them it, and advised that it was the same glass she had used, and the waiter assured him it was. He said it likely had the drug he used on Ina. He asked Ina to play the video for them from her phone.

After that, two of the three officers were on their phones, and they had conversations about Tariz; they had identified who he was.

They were sketchy as it was an ongoing investigation, but likely, he was involved in human trafficking. They explained, especially with such a prime target like Ina, the grunts like Tariz would do as they were told because their rewards were very lucrative. They had read Tariz his rights and took the lamp cord off and applied handcuffs.

They explained to Garret and Ina that he would be interrogated with their own methods, and they would get to the bottom of his involvement. Garret asked about the charges against me and what would be done. They explained that after all the information, evidence, and possibly a confession from Tariz, we could expect me to be released within a day. I would have to go before a judge, and he would review and decide what the results would be.

The police advised that they go visit me at the police station, and they took Tariz away. Garret and Ina went to the police station.

I was sitting in my cell, I had cried, prayed, and was not feeling well. A guard came to my cell and led me to another room. I was thinking another round of interrogation, but jumped with joy when I saw Ina and Garret. I ran to her and hugged her like there was no tomorrow. I was crying, and so was Ina, and Garret said, 'You guys may need a room!!' They explained what had happened, and Tariz, the trishaw driver, was in custody and likely in big trouble if he did not just disappear. Garret called his wife who asked questions about their orchard fruit.

An officer came to the room and explained that I would be held overnight till a prosecutor had reviewed all the statements, facts, and evidence and the interrogation of Tariz. They explained that they had to keep Ina's phone, although it may not be admissible as evidence, but it was part of their statements.

I was so relieved with all the events, what a change from my predicament only a short time ago. Garret and Ina had to leave, and Ina assured me she was in good hands and they would come as soon as I could be released.

April 15, near noon, a guard came to my cell and explained I had to go before a prosecutor and judge to hear the results of the investigation and charges against me. I was led into a courtroom, and the formalities of identification and such were completed, and the charges were read. The judge asked me to tell him everything, starting with the Georgetown experience and from that point on.

When I was done, he explained that he had reviewed the other statements, the evidence, the confession of the accused Tariz, and all the charges against me would be dropped. I would be released, and I can sign the release documents before him.

I approached the bench and complied. He apologized on behalf of the citizens and courts of Thailand about this serious incident, but his law enforcement personnel were just doing their job. He was smiling and finished with a comment that all my possessions would be returned except the marijuana.

I only then noticed that Garret and Ina were in the courtroom, and Ina was crying again. They took me to another area and I was returned all my possessions and Ina's phone, less the marijuana. When I was let out of a different door, they were there to greet me, and Ina hugged me so hard, taking my breath away. I did not realize just how strong she was. I gave Ina her phone back, and she asked to be excused. She had not contacted her parents and needed to update them and find out their location and travel plans.

I had been too busy wrapped in Ina's arms and chatting with her between kisses before she stepped aside to talk with her parents on her phone. It was then that I noticed a woman standing beside Garret, and I realized it must be his wife. She was laughing and said they had never had visitors like us before. She hugged me and said, 'Welcome to Thailand.'

Ina was off to the side of us and was chatting with her parents for some time in her native Swedish. She came back and told us they were currently in Frankfurt, changing planes, and had another stop in Saudi Arabia and would arrive the next day. They would text or e-mail their arrival and flight information.

She said both her parents, Lars and Ingrid, were coming. Lars was relieved that the situation was resolved, as he did not know if he could have helped, a criminal lawyer or not. Ingrid was worried sick about Ina, but both were relieved and now looking forward to this impromptu trip. They never knew where Chang Mi was or had ever been to Thailand.

We went to Garrett's car and travelled to their home. We arrived at their small orchard and his wife asked if we were hungry. Thai people do love to eat, and she had a feast prepared fit for a king. The catching up on everything in our lives was nonstop for hours, along with a few beers, although Garret did not drink.

Garret does not mince words much, and when Ina was busy with his wife Anong, he asked how much I was paying Ina. I realized he was serious, and in Thailand, this is not uncommon for a man to pay for a woman to accompany him. Garret did not know that I had been traveling with her for two months as he still thought I had been bullshitting him when I e-mailed.

I told him the background of the meeting with Ina and what we had been through on our travels. I told him about the rest of our

116

travel plans, including going back to Sweden to meet her parents. He thought she was nuts to think of keeping an old geezer like me.

Ina had come in with a tray of food and heard the last comment. She set the tray down, sat on my lap, and said she was taking her chances. She said, 'He pulled my tooth in Australia,' showed him the hole, and Garret laughed at that and was stuck for words. Ina never flaunted her beauty, and Garret told her she was like a movie star and could do much better. It was all in good fun, and we carried on just as if we were normal!! We ate and visited till late, and Ina and I were tired from our flight and ordeal, so we begged to retire.

Our bedroom was in a little cabin off from the main house, Garret said we keep it for the riff-raff. Ina did not know this expression, and I said it meant important people, but I think she did not believe me. We slept great after a rambunctious bout of sex.

April 16 in the morning, Anong had a Thai breakfast ready, and Garret had plans to visit a number of the sites around Chang Mi. Chang Mi is a very old city with many well-preserved temples. We went to the WR Pra Tat Doi Sutheo and the Wat Chedi Loang, which really show the traditional Lanna and Buddhist cultures.

We stopped for lunch at a restaurant that specialized in Khoa Sol, a creamy curry-based noodle soup topped with crispy fried noodles. We also had some Sai Oua, a spicy herb sausage. We had a couple of Siam Surray, a tasty cocktail that uses some of the same ingredients as Tom Yum soup. We visited a couple more temples; we only saw a small portion of the many in Chang Mi.

There is never a memory that is ingrained into us with more meaning than when something goes wrong. This series of events is as serious as anyone would never want to endure, and thankfully, it had turned out ok, with the quick and very thoughtful actions of my friend Garret and my travel mate Ina.

Ina's parents' flight was due to arrive later in the evening. Oh boy, I would meet her parents, who must be thinking what kind of smuck Ina is mixed up with. We had the day to relax and catch up with Garret and Anong about so many things.

Ina would often just come to me and hug me like there is no tomorrow, and cried often, she was still very upset about the events, and likely was flashing ahead to what her fate may have been. We went for a walk through Garret and Anong's orchard and were just so happy to be in this position today compared to two days ago.

Garret drove us to the airport to pick up Lars and Ingrid. We were at the arrival gate, and when they came through, Ina ran to embrace both of them. I could see the worry and concern on their faces. They were reserved when greeting me, as they must have been thinking of my age and the situation. Ina was rattling away in

Swedish to them, and they were standing there in wonderment about her story.

They looked at me, and then we realized they had not met Garret. After another few minutes of her rapid-fire Swedish conversation with them, Lars shook Garrett's hand and thanked him for his help. It was easy to see where Ina got her good looks from, as her mother was as stunning a lady as you can find in her mid-sixties, I assumed. My twisted mind was saying I have the wrong lady, yikes.

Lars looked at me with an expression I was not sure what kind of, because he had just heard a story about the possible disappearance of his daughter, and I was involved and probably could have prevented it.

Ingrid was quite quiet and was not looking at me. I think she was trying to digest everything and was possibly as relieved as her husband.

We collected their bags and drove to Garrett's orchard. Ina never stopped talking to Lars and Ingrid, and I stayed quiet as this was very shaky ground for me. What a disastrous way to meet my possible future in-laws. Ina was gaining ground, I think because Ingrid hugged her and they stayed that way for a while.

"Thai Minefields and Scoundrels"

After arriving at Garrett's and Anong's orchard, they met Anong and I was hoping they would settle down from the hellish emotions. To have me in custody and possibly charged and convicted of a crime was one thing, but to learn of the bastard Tariz's involvement and the possible results of that was very scary. I am sure they were thinking her choice of a travel partner was not the best.

Anong had a spread laid out for a gang, and we all dug in to eat. Garret had Sangsom Thai rum with soda and some of the local beer. I found that both Lars and Ingrid liked the rum and likely needed it. They were so relieved by the turn of events for the better that they were letting their hair down a little. Ina had sat on my lap a few times and would hug and kiss me fiercely; her mother took notice of this and was still quiet, and I assumed she was not approving.

As the conversation drifted to our trip before the disaster in Georgetown, I noticed Ingrid and Lars looking at me differently. I did not think they could just erase the possible dire straits their daughter and I had been in. They would take time to adjust and accept me, if they ever would. Swedish people can be very proper and formal. They were loosening up as the night progressed.

Lars and Ingrid were quite tired from their jet lag and time change. Ina and I gave them the cabin, and they retired for the night. Garret and I had memories about our times in Canada, and he asked lots of questions about Les. Anong and Ina got along very well, and I could tell Anong appreciated the help in serving and cleaning up.

Ina and I had a quiet night together, just so relieved to be together, and I told her many times how sorry I was. I tried to suggest that our travels had been so safe, and we had a fantastic time in New Zealand, where we met, Australia was a blast, Barry and Liberty's time together in the Philippines was super, and then we had our guard down. I explained that people in this part of the world do not consider life as important as in our countries. People exploit their family and friends for monetary gain.

Ina did not agree with me, she thinks that people everywhere in the world are good, but I said yes, there are many good people the world over, but there are always the bad eggs. Tariz is the example of that, he appeared so friendly and helpful but was a scumbag planner with the intention to exploit Ina and make money from it, while putting me in a prison for something I did not do.

She had never experienced this in any other part of the world and was naive about it. She did not blame me, but I disagreed, as my travels to many places had taught me that in foreign countries in Asia, the Middle East, Africa, and South America, a traveller must keep their guard up against people who will exploit others. I related only a few of the stories my brother had experienced in his long journey to all the continents and sixty countries.

April 17, I hoped, would bring some resolve to the nightmare that Ina, I, Garret, Lars, and Ingrid had all been through. Anong had a traditional Thai breakfast of Khao tom boiled rice with egg) and Sai ua (a grilled pork spicy sausage) with strong coffee. She also had tasty flat bread, almost like a pancake with nuts and chocolate in it, and a local honey with a berry taste. She has a beekeeper with hives in their orchard where the honey comes from.

Lars and Ingrid had slept in quite late with jet lag bothering them. Once up, Anong fed them this hearty breakfast, and we all sat around chatting again for hours. They had recovered some and were excited to see some of the temples and sites Chang Mi was famous for.

I mostly kept quiet, I did not feel comfortable with Ingrid, she still looked at me very little, and I knew she was not accepting me yet. Ina was talkative as ever, relating our travels before Singapore, and as all her stories were positive, the mood was better.

Since it was afternoon, Garret took us around Chang Mi to only four temples, and we had a traditional supper out at his favorite restaurant.

Our meal started with a Kao Soi, a Chinese soup handed down recipe from the "Hor" tribe near the Laos/Thai border. We had grilled Sai oas, Khao niao mauang, Pad Thai, Kao soi, all with sticky rice and hot sauces to boost the already hot flavour of most of the dishes. There was so much to eat, we were all stuffed and finished with the Thai black tea, either hot or with ice. We all had a great time, and the conversations were happy, and everyone was constantly laughing.

When we returned to Garrett's and Anong's house, Garret was able to download Ina's and my phone photos, and Ina and I narrated them, and we answered lots of questions.

Ina related the story where I basically attacked the drunk who was bothering her, and she was angered that she had not used her jujitsu.

The story of the opal Ina had found and the underground hotel owners' betting and winnings were cause for many cheers and were saluted with some Thai rum. Ina explained that the opal was being cut and made into identical rings for her and Ingrid and would be sent to her apartment in Sweden.

Ina explained the tooth episode and showed her parents the hole. Ingrid was flabbergasted that she could let me do that, and why not find a dentist? Ina explained that where we were, there were no dentists, but an old guy, Fred, would have pulled it. Ina explained that we got penicillin in Alice Springs, and the infection had cleared up. Ingrid said that it is the same tooth that was bothering her back home, and when she goes back, she will get an implant for it.

Lars had lots of questions for me about the VW van as he and Ingrid had travelled around Europe in one when Ina was conceived. Ina did not know this, and they were reliving things that sometimes just stay buried till circumstances brought them up.

It was already a much better atmosphere, especially with Ina, me, and her parents. Ingrid would sometimes ask me questions also, like about the young rambunctious cliff jumpers who we camped beside, Ina said she was not concerned, she had her ju jitsu, but she said the old man just gets respect with his attitude and what he says, they knew they could and would not mess with him.

Lars asked Garret if he was like a James Bond spy with his talent and technique with the bastard kidnapper, as he called Tariz. Garret is quiet and humble about his abilities and suggested that he would only do what was right. He said he is not fond of inflicting pain, but if the situation required it, he would only do so when he resorts to this.

Ina commented that she had not practised much jujitsu for years, and the state of her ability to react would need to be addressed. Garret offered to take her to his club, and his instructor would evaluate and help her.

Because of the many cheers and salutes with rum and beer to photos and stories, we were all quite happy and tired. Ina and I curled up and slept like logs, content and happy.

April 18, Ina crept out of bed as soon as Anong was up and helped with breakfast. Lars and Ingrid were up early, still having some jet lag but ready to see more of this paradise they called Chang Mi. We visited another six temples, took a boat trip to a floating bazaar where we ate from the vendors along the way. Ingrid and Ina were so busy shopping that Lars was constantly packing bags for them. Garret often just sat in his car and waited for us to finish our tours; he could see these sites every day.

Back at their orchard, Anong had a Thai spread laid out that surpassed the meal we had the night before with some different tastes. Lars and Ingrid were so thankful to Anong that Ingrid presented her with a special Buddha that Garret had suggested she had her eye on for a while. She was in tears and hugged Ingrid, they were sharing recipes, and Ingrid was helping Anong in the kitchen. Everyone was beat from a busy day, and with a few of the Thai rums we were all settled for the night.

There had been little discussion about the travel plans of Lars and Ingrid; they had an unknown routing or timing for their return flights. Ina and I had not thought about our plans with all the events that had occurred.

April 19, in the morning, Ina and I were still in bed, and we were called to breakfast. Ingrid was up and helping Anong. Ina was so surprised at this that she kissed her mother and hugged her. She told me she had never seen her so interested in cooking, and her relationship with Anong surprised Ina.

Garret told Ina to eat light as they had a visit to his club and she would need an empty stomach. He would drop her there and return to tour us more. Lars and Ingrid declined as they were content to relax. Garret was happy; he was able to stay with Ina for the jujitsu session.

Lars and Ingrid expressed that they wanted to talk with me alone. I was worried this may be a discussion where they would try to see what my intentions were and dissuade me from anything to do with their daughter. Ina had been talking to them in Swedish before they left, and I knew it was about me.

Lars mostly carried the talking for them, and he started by asking a little more about my background, my parents, growing up, and my career, kind of feeling me out. He asked if I thought I was taking advantage of Ina. I asked that he speak to her about that, but I certainly did not think so; she had a choice in everything we did together, she never expressed any concerns, we had such a fantastic trip till arriving here, it was like a fairy tale.

I expressed my disgust at myself for not recognizing the scum that Tariz turned out to be, I knew better and being the trip had been so good, I was too comfortable, my travel guard was down. They agreed, but Ingrid was not sure she could ever forget this transgression, and what about the future?

I was not sure what she meant, but she wanted to talk about any further travel plans we had. She told me Ina had not told her what we planned, and they are concerned that we may get into circumstances like this again. I told her that the rest of our plans were to fly to New Delhi, then Kathmandu in Nepal, and hike into a meditation and yoga retreat for 2-3 weeks in the Himalayas. She asked me where I got the ideas for my travel plans. I explained what my brother had done.

On my phone, I brought up the story I had written about his four-year and one hundred and seventy-day trip. They were quite surprised, and Ingrid asked if I had written this. I said certainly, but not published as it is too short, and I do not know if it is a marketable quality. Ingrid was quiet, reading the index and prologue. She was reading, and I waited quite patiently, not sure what was going on. Lars was quiet, sitting, sipping his now-quite favorite Sangsom Thai rum on ice.

Ingrid finished the first chapter, I think, and she asked me again if I wrote this. I said yes, most certainly. She asked me how many chapters, and Lars just 'harumphed' into his drink, which caused Ingrid to look at him. She said, 'Lars, I don't know this guy from Adam, so I want to see if he is real.' Swedes can be quite formal and even boring, so I waited patiently.

She sort of flashed through my story on my phone by scrolling down, stopping now and then to read a bit, she got to the bottom, and was scrutinizing the map. She stood up, came to my chair, and said, Can you explain this map. I turned it the right way up, as it is upside down on my phone, and retraced Les's trip.

She stood there and said, 'My God, he did that.' She read the title, 'Travel the world in Four Years and One Hundred and Forty Days.' Is this real? I said, 'Certainly, he was my brother,' and I told her a little more about our time living together when he returned.

Lars was quiet as ever, got up to replenish his rum, and when he looked at me, he raised his eyebrows and winked. I was not sure about the direction this was taking. Ingrid sat down and continued to scroll through my story again. She looked at me and said, 'About 12,000 words, it is a short story.'

I looked at Lars, and he spread his arms, like she is all yours, buddy. She was thinking and asked me how I got to New Zealand from Canada. I told her, and she said so, 'From what I have gathered, you may be retracing his route.' I smiled and said, 'Well, only part of it this trip and not every part of his trip on this portion, mainly because of Ina.'

She looked at me and asked, 'What did you say you did for a living?' Again, I was not sure where this conversation was going, so I said, 'I am a civil engineer and did that all my career.'

She said, 'Did you ever consider writing?' I told her about my 45000-word story about my Family Farm history and the reason why I had written it. Then I wanted to honor my brother's trip and wrote that. Now I am making notes about this trip I am on.

She was very intrigued, and I could not quite put my finger on the reason. Finally, she looked at me and said, 'She is the chief editor/publisher of a Publishing company called Bonnierforlagon – Bonner Books.' Oh, I said, 'So you know lots about writers and books.' She was apologetic about not telling me, she said she just got into a work mode when she looked at my story.

Lars was smiling like a big cat curled up on a chair. He looked at Ingrid and said, 'Maybe we should get back on our topic of discussion.' Ingrid smiled at him, and I told them that I must speak about myself and Ina.

They were both quiet and waiting. I explained that I never intended to take advantage of Ina; the way we met and how our relationship progressed was completely unexpected and surprising. I told them that we rarely discussed anything to do with our long-range plans, we both were just going with the flow of two travellers, accommodating mostly my route plans, based on, yes, my brother's trip.

I explained that I had bought the van in Sydney as it was part of my travel plans to duplicate my brother's experience. I was not a rich man, but I had plenty of funds for this trip and maybe more for his journey. I never expected or asked Ina to share the cost of the van.

When we arrived at Darwin and spoke with you, we decided to fly directly to the Philippines, bypassing the Indonesian islands. It was partly safety, partly logistics, and partly duration.

I told them that my friends Barry and Liberty had only arrived there, but I could have stayed at their house anyway. I explained Singapore, Malaysia, Thailand (here at Garret and Anong's orchard), then India and Nepal were all planned to meet her schedule to return to her career.

I explained that my nephew's ex-wife, Su, in Hat Yai, Thailand, is very much a telepathic mind reader, a mental telepathist, and she initiated Ina and me to address our future. We had a very long discussion that night after visiting Su, and we talked for a long time about our love for each other and possible long-range plans that would include me coming to Sweden after Nepal.

I explained that part of that discussion, I expressed to Ina that I am old, she is young, but it did not sway her love for me or her plans for us together in the future. Lars and Ingrid were quiet and thinking. I told them Ina and I agreed to talk about this more and decide what to do in Nepal. I asked them what they were thinking; Ingrid wanted to go for a walk with Lars.

The length of our discussions had been a couple of hours, and I was very surprised when Anong walked into the room. She is a patient person and has not interfered with my discussion with Lars and Ingrid. She sat down and asked how our talk went. I explained what had happened, and she said, Just be patient----- she knows Ina loves me. She asked if I loved her, and I said most certainly, but was worried about our age separation. She said, 'Do not worry, it will work out.'

Garret and Ina arrived back, and Ina took one look at me and asked where Lars and Ina were. I told them we had a long chat, and they went for a walk. She looked quite worried and asked Anong about the chat. Anong just smiled and said it was none of her business; she had a nap while they were talking. Ina was persistent, and I told her a little, but then Lars and Ingrid arrived back from their walk. They looked cheerful and wanted to sit and talk some more.

We all sat together, and Garret and Anong left us alone. This time, Ingrid did most of the talking. She started by suggesting that we have a good talk, and she now understands better why Ina and I are travelling together and why we chose our destinations and durations. She explained that she was initially terrified about the possible plight of Ina, not caring about me, as she thought I was responsible. After she knew the facts and circumstances, she did not blame me; she was so relieved it worked out.

She asked Ina if she was having second thoughts about me after the events that took place. Ina suggested that we were in that together, and we needed to support each other and be more aware in the future.

Ingrid asked Ina about our age difference, and Ina told her that she is totally aware of this and it does not matter; she loves me very much. Ina said that it was she who initated our first sex, and I had asked her at the time if she was sure what she was doing.

Lars and Ingrid laughed at that and commented that Ina has a stubborn mind of her own and often proves it. Ingrid asked if we would have open minds about our relationship because of the age difference, but she and Lars are behind us all the way.

It was a huge relief to hear this from Ingrid. Lars sat there sipping his rum like a cat lost its tongue, and he said he knew when to be quiet when a Swedish woman is speaking her mind. I chimed in that I have experienced that with another Swedish woman. We were all laughing, and a round of Thai rum was in order.

Both Ingrid and Ina went to help Anong in preparing supper. Garret, Lars, and I took a walk in the orchard, and Garret was explaining all the fruits and the difficulties with the orchard, mostly involving a lack of water at critical times. Lars was asking about where the produce is sold, and Garret explained that it is mostly local, with vendors that come to pick and then sell. He said he is getting by, but it was not a great money maker.

Anong had prepared a small pig, and we roasted it out on the patio on a spit. Garret had dried fruit tree chips to smoke the pig with. Supper was special as the air had cleared and part way through, Ingrid proposed a toast to the new couple at the table and wished us the best of luck.

She also announced that there is a possible new writer in our midst, and this surprised Ina. Ina asked what she meant, and she explained that I showed her the story of my brother's trip and how it is only a short story, but maybe with books 2,3 & 4 it could be a bestselling novel??

Ina looked at me and asked if I knew what her mother did, and I said I do now after our talk. Ingrid said that from what little she had read, she thinks the Swedish people and many more will eat this story up. She only read a bit, but when I send it to her today, she will read it all.

Ina commented to beware, she is a bear of an editor, and she will chew your writing to bits till you get it right.

Garret was the same quiet old geezer I knew from back in Canada, and I proposed a toast to the James Bond in our midst.

Ina commented that Garret and his instructor gave her thumbs up, but she commented she aches all over and will take up her jujitsu again to polish up her skills after the embarrassing session with them. Garret said she will not need a lot of polishing, and she is as strong as a tiger; Ike must attest to that. This brought a cheery round of laughing and comments.

What a great day for friends, new and old, for some, possibly new in-laws, and stories and experiences that will be right up there as some of the best in my life. Lars said that Anong is not cooking in the morning as he was taking us all out to breakfast. We all retired to bed.

April 20 had us all spill into Garrett's SUV, and breakfast was a lively affair, and it stuffed us all. Lars and Ingrid expressed how thankful they were now that the trip had turned around, and both Lars and Ingrid were really glad for the impromptu trip. Ina said they were like two sticks in the mud back home, and it was fantastic to see them change with this trip.

Lars and Ingrid wanted to talk about possibly joining Ina and me travelling to New Delhi, Kathmandu in Nepal, and going into the Himalayas with us. They were here in Asia, and both had time; money was not an issue, and they thought our plan sounded exciting and intriguing.

I noticed Ina was confused because of the request. She asked Ingrid what had gotten into them. Ingrid said they were confused themselves, but thought, 'What the hell, you only live once.'

Garret and Anong were sad they could not just jump on a plane with us, but had their orchard to harvest and manage.

Ingrid and Ina were on their phones booking flights and hotels. Lars said to me, 'Min son, Du ar en bra kille (my son, you are a good guy), you just need to keep your mouth shut, let those dominating Swedish babes do their thing.' It was ironic for him to call me his son, as we were much the same age, and I thought I would have to learn the Swedish language. We were scheduled to fly out the next day, early from Chang Mi to New Delhi.

That night, we went out for a final supper together with Garret and Anong. Lars was paying for everything; he was not letting anyone pay, he was saying it was the least he could do. Back at the orchard, we all settled in for the night.

Chapter 7
"The Beauty of India"

April 21, we were up early and said our goodbyes to Garret and Anong. We had a van taxi pick us up with all the luggage. At the airport, we checked in, cleared customs and had to purchase a visa for travel into India. Ingrid was so excited, she hugged me once, and Ina scowled at her, then laughing and said, "Careful, he is all mine." I asked how these flights were paid, and Lars said, "Not to think about it, you travel with us, you do not pay."

We arrived at our seats, and to my surprise, we were in first class. I was questioning this, and Lars reminded me not to argue with a Swedish woman, just tell her you love her. The flight was pleasant as I had never ridden first class in my life. After a delicious meal and champagne, Ina and I curled up together in our double bed type of seats, and I thought I had died and gone to heaven. The flight was nearly seven hours and arrived in New Delhi on time.

When recovering our luggage, two men looked after it, and we followed them. Ingrid informed me that the hotel we were booked into provided a limousine service for us.

Wow, first class all the way, the men from the Connaught Hotel were looking after us and all the Taxi drivers left us alone really quickly. The hotel was top-of-the-line accommodation for me; I bit my tongue and told Ina, 'I love you'.

We settled into our suite, which featured a full kitchen and bar, as well as two bedrooms and a separate bathroom in each. After a visit to the spa for a massage and hot tub, we returned to our suite, where a cook arrived with a large trolley filled with an impressive array of food. The cook mixed us drinks first, and Lars just smiled and motioned to me to take a seat and drew a line across his mouth. I could tell they were used to this kind of living, and I would have to grin and bear it.

Ingrid and Ina came back from their massage, facials and hair stylist and looked gorgeous and happy. Ina seemed more formal and not as spontaneous as I often experienced with her during our travels. I realized that she had enjoyed the change in our travelling style and making do with amenities and simpler things at times. From everything I was experiencing, I thought I might not like these uppity first-class people so much.

We enjoyed a steak supper, baked potatoes and asparagus, cooked right in front of us, with an expensive wine and a fancy chocolate cheesecake dessert. After the cook cleaned up and left, we settled down, and the chit-chat again centered on portions of our trip. Ina was chatting with her Dad, and Ingrid was chatting with me.

Ingrid was curious about more of my brother's journey and experiences. She said she had Ina open my phone and send the story to her tablet, and she had read it all on the flight. It surprised me, but Ina and I were sleeping and I had paid no attention to them. She asked me who had edited it for me, and I told her no one, and I had done it myself. She said there are some small errors, but nothing too drastic.

She asked where I got all the information from, like the route, dates, and the experiences described. I explained that I had been querying my sister-in-law about writing this story, she had no issue with me doing it, and she gave me two little diaries, a survey book, a small Falcon atlas of the world and about 2000 slides. She was confused and asked where my brother was, and I told her he had passed.

I explained that some portions had day-to-day notations, while others, such as Europe, Scandinavia, the job in South Africa, and the trip from Mexico through the US, were blank. She was impressed that I could put together the kind of detail at times, and other portions, next to nothing.

She now understood that the exact excerpts I included were from his diaries. She asked why the job in South Africa, and I explained he left Canada working on a ship, worked in New Zealand, Australia, Germany and South Africa, basically worked his way around the world.

She was totally impressed with this fact and said she wished she could have met and talked to him; she could have hooked him up with writers and made him millions. She was a reader who absorbed everything she read and could recall it in detail. No wonder she is the chief editor in the company that I assumed she worked for.

I said she must read a lot of these potential stories. She smiled and said she used to, but now all her editors do that; she just supervises them. She said my company is always looking for talent, and I can recognize it.

I began to realize that she and Lars are the owners of the company, and I asked if they own the company. She said we own fifty-one per cent, which keeps control in their hands. Wow, I was travelling and talking with a multimillionaire, way above my pay scale and experience, what the hell was I doing?

Ina came to sit with me and asked what her mother and I were discussing. We both looked at her, and Ingrid said, 'I think I just found another writer. ' Lars came with a bottle of the Sangsom Thai rum he had smuggled from Thailand and not declared, and said, "Enough of business, let's have some rum." I was really taking a shine to Lars, I thought I could get along with him really good.

We talked more about our lives, and Lars and Ingrid recalled their trip around Europe with the VW van when Ina was conceived.

Ina described my trip with two Boston teachers in a VW van from Germany to southern Europe for three months.

I told them the story of my ride through Belgium and Germany, and the ride on the truck ferry with the band playing at the lounge was four youngsters called ABBA. OMG was Ingrid's expression. You saw ABBA, I said yes when they were just a bar band.

Ingrid said these are more stories in the making, and I said, "But I cannot tell everything about that eight-month trip around Europe," which brought laughs. There was a sense of peace between Lars, Ingrid, and me. They were getting to know more about me, and I hoped they were not disappointed.

We were all worn out from travel and went to bed. Ina was very rambunctious in bed, and I was concerned about the noise, but Ina said they could handle it; they had heard it before. The next morning, breakfast was cooked right before us in our suite.

April 22, Ingrid and Ina had a private guided tour arranged including: Sri Gurudwara, Bagla Sahib, Qutub Minar, Delhi, Humayun's Tomb, India Gate and the Red Fort.

We had an authentic New Delhi meal around noon and back in our suite for a late afternoon massage and hot tub. The ladies joined us this time and I felt out of place, but what could I do but keep my mouth shut.

Ingrid commented that for an old guy, I had a good body. Ina said, "Careful, mother." Lars was complaining and said, "What about his body is like?" and Ingrid, laughingly said, "Maybe you should talk to the old guy and get his secrets." We had a cooked meal in our suite again, and we all hit the sack, worn out.

In the morning, we had breakfast cooked and we were off in the limousine to Agra for a tour of the Taj Mahal and the Itmad-ud-Duala and back to our terrible digs in New Delhi. The limo ride was complete with more Sangsom Thai rum, and I chased it with beer. Boy, was life a bitch.

I prepared an email to Garret about my troubles here in New Delhi and Agra. His response was, "Enjoy it, bucko, you ride as long as you can, maybe they will dispose of you when they tire of you." He said I thought they may be a little uppity, and I was far from this class. Ride 'em, cowboy was his parting words.

The next morning, **April 23**, during our cooked breakfast in the suite, Ingrid asked me what I would like to do. I said I think I have died and gone to heaven with this lifestyle, she laughed.

I said, "I would actually like to go see some of life's reality and show you a slum." She asked what that would entail. I described some of the details about the slum my nephew had taken me to in Mumbai about ten years ago.

Lars said he would like to go, and Ina also, so Ingrid was outvoted. I explained how we dress with no jewelry, no watch, our pockets turned inside out, and they listened to me.

I said, "Give me a little time, and I will be back." I went to the front desk and inquired with the head honcho about a staff member who could take me to a slum and give me a quick tour. He thought about that. Talked on his phone for a minute, and said, "He is off in about one hour, and he will take us himself."

I think he may have changed shifts with someone, as he smelled some cash in it for himself. I explained that if he has any shenanigans in mind, I would personally kick the living shit out of him.

He wanted an explanation about shenanigans and knew what kick the living shit out of him meant. I slipped him a fifty-dollar US dollar, and as he was bowing and smiling, he said he would be ready in one hour.

I went back to the room and explained I had arranged a guide, and we will leave in and hour. When we came down to the front desk, Suraj was waiting for us and had our limo waiting.

Ingrid commented that he is the front desk boss, and I said he is happy to take us. He sat in the back with us and explained that he is very honoured to take us on this tour, but we must want to tour something other than a slum.

I told him, "Remember what I said, Suraj, he looked at me and put his hands together and bowed. Ingrid asked what our deal was, and I explained that I wanted a straight forward quick slum tour and no shenanigans, or I would kick the living shit out of him. Soraj was looking a little pale and bowing and looking down, a showing of respect and humbleness.

I asked him to tell me when we get close. I asked him how many of his family members live there, and he said many, including him. When we were close, I said, "Okay, stop about two blocks away, and we'll walk the rest." I wanted a two- to three-block circuit into the slum and back out. He understood and was on his cell phone. We got out of the limo, and the driver waited there for us. I took Ingrid's purse and gave it to the driver, and asked Lars and Ingrid to take off their wedding rings.

I think they thought this was a bit much, but they listened, and we were off. Suraj was on his phone, and we were walking parallel to a canal. Ingrid commented that there was a terrible smell in the air; I said that it was the canal.

As we neared the slum entrance, a chain link fence stretched both ways from us as far as we could see. There were about six teenage boys at the entrance, and it was obvious to me that Suraj had arranged for them.

They walked ahead on each side of us and kept the beggars, children, thieves, and dogs away from us. Each boy had a stick that delivered sharp, stinging blows where required.

The smell was as expected, which I had experienced, but not Lars, Ingrid, and Ina; Ingrid had her nose covered. The area we walked through was okay, but the side of the narrow street was lined with garbage. There were some injured and/or mutants peeking out of doorways or on the side of the street.

We turned at a corner and went about fifty feet and came to a latrine area about fifty feet long, and there were children, and adults, both males and females, urinating or crapping on the ground in front of a four-foot-high wall.

About twenty people were lined up, and at each end, a man with a shovel threw the deposits over the wall. We made it past the latrine area, turned another corner, and came back to the fence, where we had to backtrack down the fence to our entrance gate. Ingrid was walking as fast as she could with her nose covered and looking terrified.

We got back to the limo, and the driver had a bucket of disinfected water and rags, which we all washed our shoes with. I handed out sterile face cloths to wash our faces, hands, and arms. I handed out bottled water, which I told them had an antivirus additive in case we ingested anything airborne into our stomachs. When we got back, I wanted everyone to have a long steam and breathe deeply for five minutes.

I think they thought I was paranoid. We climbed back into the limo, and Suraj was only looking at the floor, and it was obvious from his embarrassment. The limo was dead silent. I broke the ice and said, "Well, I am really thirsty, and will you have a beer with me, Suraj. He looked up and gave me a big grin, accepted only water and clicked bottles with me.

I thanked him for the escort and gave him another fifty US dollars. Lars was going to give him more, but I said, "Please do not, he is already embarrassed at taking the money I gave him and what I gave him before. He just made double his month's salary. Oh no, Suraj spoke up, I do not make that much. Well then, I said, "Enjoy," and he wanted another water and looked like he had not drunk anything for weeks as he chugged it.

Ingrid was looking out the window and was deep in thought. I expected she was angry at me for forcing them to do this tour. I said, "I think you are all upset with me for suggesting this tour. I did not force you, but please let it sink in, and when you are back home and recall this short tour, you may realize just how great your life is."

"I am not trying to embarrass you or degrade you; I just want you to open your minds a little," I said. Ina was looking at me differently, trying to figure out her thoughts, accepted a beer and chugged it down, then Lars did the same, and we all broke out laughing, except Ingrid, who kept looking out the window.

Back at the hotel suite, we all sat around, and I asked Ingrid if she was angry with me. She took a while to answer, and she said she was not sure of my intentions, but said she was actually glad I had arranged this tour. She said, "It gives one the complete opposite side of what we have toured for the last week." She said,

"She would have never believed people live like that, and where were the deposits from the latrine area going?" I told her it goes into the canal, and that is what we smelled when approaching the slum.

I said India faces three main problems, and no order can be given to prioritise them; they are people (population), water, and garbage. Everyone was thinking about that, and Ingrid said, "You are not just a hillbilly country boy; you think about mankind and our problems."

I said, "Lars told me to keep my mouth shut and not to argue or question a stubborn Swedish lady. I have not, and I am going for a massage and steam bath. Anyone interested?" Ingrid threw a pillow at me, and Ina tackled me on the couch and sat straddling me while rubbing my face and pummeling me. We were all laughing and went for our massages and steam baths.

Back in our suite, Lars cancelled the in-house cooking for supper and wanted to go check out the street vendors. I called Suraj and he took us and found the best and safest vendors. Lars paid double for each thing we tried. Back in our suite, I brought out my pills to help prevent stomach issues with street food, and everyone took them without a complaint or question.

I passed out sterile wipes, and Ingrid took hers and said, "You have passed these out after almost every tour and at the end of each day, you are so thoughtful." I told her I had caught a wicked stomach bug that took weeks to recover from, and it helps to prevent that again.

Ingrid and Ina were busy booking flights from New Delhi to Kathmandu, in Nepal. I recommended the Mandala Yoga and Meditation 7-day Retreat as it will possibly have a view of Mount Everest if the weather is favourable.

Chapter 8
"Nepal Adventures"

We were booked to fly out the next day, **April 24**. I was lying in bed with Ina; she was wrapped around me and deep in thought. She said she feels so lucky to be with me, and she cannot believe her parents are here and doing everything they are. She said they seemed such sticks in the mud at home in Sweden and were so worried about her taking this trip.

Even though they were forced to come to our aid, it turns out this is breaking their mold of their boring lifestyle back in Sweden. She sees such changes in them and how they are loosening up and enjoying life instead of just making money.

We discussed that Ina's three-month leave of absence can be met, even with our 7-day retreat. She can be back a few days before returning to work. She said you will live with me in my apartment.

This hit me hard as I realized that I am committed to this wonderful lady, and my life will change drastically. Ina said she knows a specialist who can extract sperm from my tenticles and, by the in vitro method, impregnate her and she wanted to do this soon.

Holy shit, she was planning a family, was I to be a father at seventy-five years young??? Was I to shut my mouth and tell her 'yes, honey, I love you???' Sleep was difficult for me, but not for Ina, who was softly snoring.

Our flight to Kathmandu was short, and the mountainous area was breathtaking. We had a night in Kathmandu before the start of the seven-day retreat. We checked into the Barahi Hotel and enjoyed the pool and hot tub.

We had lunch at the hotel restaurant with a creamy Nepalese soup and a croissant. For the main course, we chose the yak stew with a Tongba tea. We sat in the lounge and chatted, sampling the Raksi (rice-based liquor) and Kukuri rum. Lars wanted two bottles, as they were uniquely shaped like a knife, and he likes rum. Ingrid likes to question me about my writing of the Family Farm, and she wanted a copy of that.

April 25, the Mandala passenger van picked us up at 9 am for our trip to the retreat, about one hour away in the mountains. We checked into the facility and had a vegetarian light lunch. The whole week was a vegetarian diet. We had a massage, a steam bath, and later a Yoga Niday meditation.

April 26 started with breakfast, yoga and breathing techniques, lunch, a hike to Gumba temple, healing for mental and physical relaxation techniques and supper.

April 27, breakfast, yoga and breathing, Reiki healing technique, lunch, meditation techniques, supper and relaxation.

April 28, breakfast, hiking up Gumba hill, Mount Everest was partially visible, the weather there looked nasty, a lunch on the hill, back for a massage and supper, and sleep. Ina was relaxed most days but quite randy on others, and sex was fantastic.

April 29, breakfast, yoga and breathing, sound healing techniques, lunch, Kundali meditation, steam, supper and relax. We had time each night to sit around a fire or lounge and discuss our experiences and what we enjoyed or did not enjoy. Ingrid seemed lost in another world and never stopped smiling; I think Lars had something to do with that.

April 30: Hiked and sightseeing to Monkey Temple, Hanaman Doka Durbar Square for breakfast, Boudhanath Stupa, and then to the village of Thamel, where we visited multiple shops with authentic Nepalese clothing and souvenirs. We also picked our own lunch choice and hiked back.

May 1, day 7 morning yoga with a splash of pranayama (breathing yoga), a final breakfast, check out, and our ride back to the Barahi Hotel.

We all dug into a Yak steak supper as we had no meat for seven days. We had a pool and hot tub, and we relaxed with some of the Tonga tea and Kukuri rum. We sat around and reviewed our seven-day experience.

The yoga and breathing were the favorite for Ingrid and Ina, as they had already experienced yoga. Lars and I did not do so well at yoga, but liked the meditation and massages best. We were all relaxed and almost in our own separate worlds from this experience.

Ingrid and Lars were holding hands a lot and smiling. I think their experience rejuvenated some romantic feelings, and likely, sex was great. Ina was smuggled into me and seemed as relaxed as a cat purring on a nice warm cushion.

Chapter 9
"Journey Crossroads"

I was at a difficult crossroads. I wanted to go with Ina to Sweden and start our new life. This scared me a bit. With her mother around, Ina was much more subdued and in control, unlike the spontaneous and energetic Ina I had travelled with for two months prior to her parents' arrival.

I was contemplating trying to cross Pakistan, Afghanistan, Iran, Turkey, the Balkan coast, continue through Europe and finally Sweden and my beautiful Ina.

I was thinking of taking a break from Ina, giving us both a chance to reflect on our relationship and decide if it's worth pursuing long-term. If we're serious about making it work, we should use this time to figure out how to manage our separation. I know she would push back with concern for my safety through these Middle Eastern countries, and wonder if I was questioning my love for her. How was I to approach this topic without creating a riff and possibly hurting our relationship?

Ina sensed that I was deep in thought and wanted me to share them. I asked that we go to our room, and I wanted just the two of us to share my thoughts. When settled in our room, I explained my thoughts of separating and travelling alone through the Middle East, the Balkan Coast, Europe, and then to Sweden.

She was surprised and angry and asked, "What was my problem?" Did I not enjoy her company and her parents, and did I not love her? She was not a happy camper.

I explained that I am here and may never get another chance to do this once I settle with her in Sweden. She was very concerned about my safety in the Middle East and my reasons for doing this.

She asked if her mother had suggested this plan to provide information and experiences for writing a book, the second in a series. I said no, her mother had nothing to do with this; this is my idea, maybe to honour my brother and his trip. She thought that was stupid, and at my age, I am a target and will die. She was crying.

This was our first real spat or disagreement, and it did not sit well with either of us. I asked her to sleep on it with me, and maybe we can approach her parents about this and get their thoughts on it. She didn't think that was a good idea, but she hoped her mother would agree, and Lars always listens to her.

We were both quiet, and slowly she drifted off to sleep, holding me like a vice, her subconscious taking control and wanting to keep me there.

We woke in the early morning, and she attacked me with a ferocious desire, as if it would be our last lovemaking. After we had tried to catch our breath, she was crying and said, "Don't do this dangerous trip." I was quiet, and we both knew I was going to do what I had described. She got out of bed and went to shower; she always wanted to shower with me, but not this time.

At breakfast, her mother looked at both of us and asked what the matter was. You both are quiet and look upset. Ina told her about my stupid idea of making the trip through the Middle East, the Balkans, Europe, and then Sweden. She had tears in her eyes, and Ingrid hugged her.

Lars looked at me and asked if I had any major concerns about this trip. I said yes, but I wanted to do it now, while I'm here, and may never have another chance. He said, "Why don't you come to Sweden and settle down with Ina, then come back here and do the trip.

I explained that I had some concerns with this lifestyle, with then paying for everything, and I was following along like a good puppy. His advice had been that the stubborn Swedish woman is in control, just go with the flow, 'Yes, honey, I love you."

I said I do not dislike their choices and lifestyle, it is a little hard to accept because my whole life has been very different. I said they would likely set us up in a house, and everything would be lovely in the garden.

Lars was puzzled and said, 'What garden?" I explained what the phrase meant, and everyone laughed, but I thought they did see my point.

Ingrid had been quiet, and she said she was so surprised at Ina's choice of travelling with me, and then the experience with the trouble in Thailand, and then our travels together with them were all a lot to digest and accept. She said Ina has a troubled heart at the moment and maybe thinks you do not love her. I said, "No I am totally committed to her and we even discussed having a family, at least two." Ina laughed and said, "I never said two, but if that's what you want, I'm okay with that."

Lars was smiling and said maybe he would go with me and we can watch each other's ass, and Ingrid was laughing at him, she said, "Your ass is much bigger, but you may lose sight of Ike's ass."

There was no consensus of opinion, but the topic was out there for all to ponder with. Ingrid and Ina wanted to be alone, and Lars and I would go for a walk.

Lars told me that when they received the call from Ina, they didn't know the full story and were just planning to take her home. He did not know anything about me and expected the worst, that Ina had made a poor choice, but would try to help me. When the situation for you was settled, we were relieved about that; it was only then that we realized how serious Ina's potential plight had been, and we were still not sure about you.

As we spent the last two weeks with you, we have gotten to know a little more about you, and I understand how you feel about our position in the world and, consequently, our lifestyle. Yes, we are privileged, and may I say we were not always this wealthy and privileged? We both have worked hard to achieve our goals, nothing was given to us, and we feel entitled to our lifestyle. Some things on this unexpected trip have opened our eyes and minds to what is going on in the world around us; we have lived in a cocoon and mostly ignored some of the world's issues.

Lars said he wanted the best for Ina; her choice was not at all what they expected. But she is a strong-willed woman, and she is also used to getting her way. Lars said, "I've noticed a change in her." She listens more and seems quite happy, and I think your love for each other is the cause of that. I was very surprised by Lars's analysis of the circumstances and issues.

We were back at the hotel, and Ingrid and Ina were waiting for us in the lounge. It was obvious that they both had been crying and had determined looks on their faces. Ina got up and gave me a big hug and kiss. She said her mother would like us all to have a chance to speak our minds about the issues.

Ingrid reached across the table separating us, and offered me her hand; I held her hand and was expecting a lecture of sorts. She looked into my eyes and said, "I want what's best for Ina, and although I had my doubts, I think you are what is best for Ina."

She explained that Ina has explained she never revealed Lars and her careers or their wealth to you. You offered shared travel costs, you never forced her to do anything she did not want to do, you respected her, you taught her many things she would never believe to do or could do, you always had her safety in mind, you are a great lover always with respect for her desires and you declared your love for her.

I was waiting for the 'but'. Ingrid continued that they did not consider your feelings and thoughts about them paying for everything, and more or less taking charge of managing many things.

When you suggested the slum tour, I was initially against it, but with everyone going, how could I say no? When we passed the latrine, I was sick and wanted to run out of there, you and your arranged tour guide and protectors were calm, and it was planned like you had done this before, and you had everything taken care of. Although the experience disgusted me and I feared the filth and potential contact with viruses, you had that planned. You washed our shoes and passed around cleansing clothes. You are a resourceful and thoughtful man.

She said I respect your choice to complete the journey of your brother as you described. I fear for your safety, as that part of the world has changed drastically since 1967. I can see you are able to look ahead and plan things accordingly; you are a determined man and a survivor. I wish you luck, and I cross my fingers we will see you in Stockholm.

Lars was next, and he said he had already talked about his concern for my safety, where I was going, and laughing, he would parachute into an Afghan or Iranian prison to help me out. He told me that he differs with me about them helping Ina out by buying us a house; she has refused help since she has been on her own, and I do not see that changing. He said he wants a grandchild. He also wished me luck.

Ina was looking at her feet. She got up and was walking back and forth, collecting her thoughts. She said she has tried to dissuade me from this trip. She knows I love her and want to spend my life with her. She realizes how the past two weeks' experience of her and her mother's dominance could annoy me, and she did not consider much about my feelings. She knows I created some humour in circumstances where I may have expressed different thoughts.

She said our two months together have been the best of her life; she has never felt more alive and in control. I've either helped her learn something new or let her figure it out on her own.

She respected my sharing of everything financially. She said when I bought the VW van, I just wanted to call dad and have him buy it, but I never asked her to share this cost, as I must have enough money of my own. She said I never questioned her about her or her family's finances; she said it's obvious that he takes care of himself.

She does not blame me for the issues with that bastard kidnapper and was amazed at my friend's resourcefulness.

She said she actually wants to be with me to watch my ass, and I can watch her ass, although he already does that, and this brought a laugh. She respects my determination and desire to complete retracing my brother's journey, although in portions with each time frame, not as long, and with far more resources. She thinks that my brother and I must have been close because every time I described something about him or his trip, it was with great respect.

She started to cry and said I do not want him to go, but I must let him do this. I know he will make it back to me, and we can start our new life. I stood up, and she hugged and kissed me like there was no tomorrow.

I guess it was my turn, because all eyes were on me. I looked at everyone slowly, settling on Ina. I told her," I love you very much, you are what anyone dreams about, but she is the real thing." "Ina is a smart and resourceful lady. I know even with our age difference, we can make it work." "Don't just close the door on that house, Ina," everyone laughed.

I told them that yes, I respected my brother, and it is kind of like a legacy for him to complete retracing his journey. I told them that Ingrid has put a challenge into my mind about completing a series of short stories about these different sections of his journey. I said I had thoughts about not completing some of the sections and writing fiction about them, but here I am on one of them. But why not plan to do them all?

I suggested that maybe on each section, "find a different Ina, would end up with four of them." This made Ina laugh and tackle me onto a couch, sitting on me. She knew I was joking.

I said I am thankful they were all giving me this chance to do this, and I will see them all in Stockholm. We had a foursome hug, and there were tears in the ladies and my eyes.

Lars suggested we go to our rooms and freshen up for supper and come to their room for a Kakuri Rum to celebrate a new beginning in our family. During our drinks, Ingrid asked me how I would handle money for this trip. I said travelling through this route is difficult as you never want much money on you.

You need the country currency you are in when exiting that country, and the country currency for the next country you are entering, and some US dollars as well. I explained that in isolated border crossings, bribes may be required both for entry and exit. I will also have three different credit cards, always my passport, and money is on my waist, never leaves there.

I explained that I never indicated to Ina, but there is a chip sewn into one inside seam on her and my backpacks. That can be pinged on with a locator from authorities if either of us goes missing. I had told Garret about this, and his police friends could have used it to track Ina, but we did not need to with Garrett's quick thinking and actions. Ina said, "You and Garret are just like James Bond and his helper."

I advised that for this next part of this trip, I plan to take bus and train travel most of the time, but a taxi could be required in a pinch. I did not want to be caught walking somewhere in difficult areas. When I reach Turkey or the Balkans, I may purchase a small car or a motorcycle for my travel mode.

Lars suggested motorcycles are dangerous, I told them I have many years of experience and have travelled about 150,000 miles on bikes. I would have to purchase proper motorcycle gear, and rain is always a pain, and I am not a young man, so a small car may be a better choice. The auto purchase with cash is best, but the license and insurance are tricky; bribes sometimes work. Ina suggested that, depending on the time, maybe she could come and meet me to travel through Europe.

Ingrid said you have done a lot of bribing, I said only when necessary and very carefully. I told them that the van driver from Malaysia, I had bribed and I was surprised when the dog in the van was pulled away from my bag; the driver likely bribed the dog handler. I should have clued in at that point and checked my bag. I said, "Now my danger antenna is up big time and I will be fine.'

I think to them it sounded like a pointless cause, but to me it was important to follow my brother's entire route, and I knew at some point I would go down Africa and across to South America.

Supper out at The Grill Restaurant, we all had tenderloin, still craving meat after a week of a vegetarian diet. The atmosphere was more jovial, as I think our family discussions had cleared the air.

Ina was quiet, and I saw her watching me much more than usual. I think she was dreading our separation. It still feels surreal that, considering how we met and started as travel companions, we've found ourselves in love and planning a future together.

After supper, we were back in our rooms for possibly our last night together. Ina was holding me like she would never see me again. We showered together, the full moon time was on Ina again. She fell asleep in my arms, and I had difficulty sleeping. What was I doing?

May 3, we all flew together from Kathmandu to New Delhi. At the airport, Ina, Ingrid, and Lars had connecting flights to Saudi Arabia, Germany, and Sweden, so our separation was beginning. Lars and Ingrid said their goodbyes, wishing me safe travels, and told me to call them if in any trouble at all.

Ina and I stood off to the side, hugging and kissing, as our parting was tearful and difficult. I assured her I was looking forward to our life together, and I would see her in Stockholm. She left with her parents and was crying, I felt like a smuck.

Chapter 10
"India, Pakistan Horrors"

I left the airport with just my backpack, about one thousand US dollars, fifty thousand Indian rupees, seventy-five thousand Pakistani rupees in cash, my credit cards, and my identification. I took a cab from the airport to the train station and bought a ticket to Dhawan Colony, near the India-Pakistan border—a crossing noted in my brother's journal, indicating it was isolated and likely would require bribes.

The train ride was crowded, as most trains in India are, but this first portion had no chickens, pigs or goats. An Indian man attempted to chat with me several times, but I ignored him as much as I could. On the last portion of the train ride, there were a few chickens and pigs that passengers brought on the train with them. The ride took about 8 hrs, and we arrived at **Dhawan Colony on May 4.** I booked a room at the Hotel Mini Mehal. There were very nice rooms and the food at their in-house restaurant was great. I sent an e-mail to Ina detailing my day 1.

I had a good sleep, and with breakfast included, I left with a full stomach. I took a tuk tuk to the bus station and bought a ticket to the Pakistan border.

Please refer to Chapter One for the border crossing details.

I was taken to one of the trucks and put into the back. The man from the train told me his name was Amar and he would accompany me back to India, and we would travel to New Delhi. He advised me that if I, at any time, attempted to escape or harm him, Richa would be harmed and possibly killed.

I tried to reason with the leader before, and was now talking to Amar. The leader came into the truck box with us and swatted me on the side of my head with his pistol. The blow knocked me on my side, and my head was cut and hurt like hell. He explained that I cannot question them or Amar about any of this affair, and if we did not do as we were told, either I or Richa would be killed.

I had little choice but to follow instructions. With the terrorizing techniques and my fear of my own and Richa's fate, I had not thought about the famous actor's mother, Shalha Chadha, whom I had met many years ago in Mumbai, India. Then it dawned on me, this young captive woman was Shalha Chadha's daughter. I recalled Shalha had lots of money, a very expensive home in Mumbai, and a country estate outside of Mumbai.

During a conversation with her many years ago at the party in Mumbai, she had told me these things and was inquiring about coming to Canada to buy land. She was loaded, and that is why these terrorists were trying to force ransom money from her in exchange for her daughter.

I was wondering what the authorities and military were doing about this kidnapping. It seemed like it should be a big thing, so where were they? I assumed that they were looking in India for the kidnappers, and little did they know that Richa was in Pakistan. There was little I could do about this. I thought it best that I just follow orders and act completely humble, scared and complacent; maybe they would not tie me up or swat me with a pistol again.

Richa was put in the back of the other truck, and about half the gang of thugs left. Amar and the leader spoke to me about their plans: I would be taken back to India, Richa's mother would be contacted and advised of the demands, and arrangements would be made for me to receive the money. After I had delivered the money to the leader, Richa would be returned to India.

The entire plan was so full of holes, I was pretty sure I would not come out of this alive and likely Richa would be killed also. My attempts to talk with them had resulted in a blow to the side of my head, so I did not want to question their plans again.

Amar and four gang members were left with me, and we traveled most of the night on back trails and roads. I had no clue where we were. The country was new to me, and it was dark.

On May 5, we were on a road that made me think we might be near the border, and the terrain looked familiar. We came to a small village, took back alleys to a house, and the jeep was pulled into a warehouse.

Inside, they had all my belongings, and a very clean and upstanding-looking man was waiting. He greeted me and told me that I would spend the next couple of hours in the trunk of his car, and that Amar and he would travel across the border. My hands were tied together, and I was told to stay quiet; at all times, I was reminded Richa's life was in danger.

They fed me some cheese, bread, and water. I was taken to a bathroom and allowed to use the toilet and wash up. This new guy asked if I understood that I was to keep quiet and whether they needed to gag me. I agreed with them and went along with everything they instructed me to do and assured them that I would be quiet.

They helped me climb into the trunk, and we were on our way immediately. The car was newer, and I had nothing to do but try to stay comfortable and relax. I actually slept some because the night had been long with travel in the jeep.

I assumed after about one hour we were at the border because I could hear people talking, and there was a lot of noise. We were on our way shortly after, and about two hours later, they stopped inside another building and got me out of the truck.

The new guy explained that we would travel about five to six hours to New Delhi, and a meeting was set up. I was to use my backpack to put the ransom money into. They would give me all the details as soon as we arrived.

We arrived at New Delhi in the evening, and we pulled into another building. There were two more men there, and both looked like they were carrying guns, and I thought they looked like police. The one spoke perfect English and informed me that I would be dropped near a clothing store, and I was to enter and ask for the manager, tell them I was there to pick up a delivery.

They dropped me about one block away, told me where the store was. When I entered the store, I told the clerk I was there to pick up a package. The clerk looked confused, likely not speaking English, and a man immediately came out of the back and told me to follow him.

We went into a back room and he took my backpack. He went out of that room and came back in about five minutes and gave me my pack back. It was considerably heavier.

I was told to go out from the back, and follow Amar; he would lead me, and I was to stay behind him a little distance away, but don't lose him. Amar was waiting about fifty feet away and turned and started walking. He went around a corner, and about three shops down, he entered a coffee shop and went straight through. In the back, he checked the bag and smiled, telling me everything was good and to keep following him.

I could never retrace this path. We went through multiple alleys and buildings, and we arrived at a warehouse. I had noticed the two burly police looking men were often near and watching everything. The same car was there, and my backpack was taken, and along with it, I was put in the trunk again.

Now I was seriously afraid for my life. They used me as the mole to carry the money because I was a white traveler; the police would not suspect me to be involved.

I had been thinking if there was some way to alert Garret about the pin locator sewn on an inside seam of my backpack. The kidnapper group would not know this. They had the money, and now, why would they leave me or Richa alive? Maybe they still needed me to cross the border with my backpack and all the money. If I were caught, it would be my neck, not theirs.

May 6. I was not far from wrong because after about 3-4 hours, we were in a city by the noise and arrived inside a building.

It was a different location again, and I was sitting on a chair. Amar told me that I would play the hitchhiking backpacker and cross the border with the upstanding-looking driver of the car.

I was angry and said that I had got them the money. Why don't they release Richa and me? They looked at me with sad eyes, and I knew my fate.

I wondered if the border where we had crossed had been strengthened because of the incident days ago, where the guard was killed. I had no clue where we were. We travelled another 3-4 hours, and we were approaching a border.

This was not the same border crossing as where, days earlier, the attack had occurred. We stopped in a village in sight of the border, and Amar was cautioning me about not doing anything stupid. The 2 thugs, looking like police officers, were with us and would be in a vehicle right behind us.

Shit, my guts were turning. If I weren't successful crossing the border, I could spend a long time in a prison in India or Pakistan, an awful scenario. Amar was in the back seat of the car, and he advised that a gun was pointed at my back at all times.

We approached the border, and leaving was no issue; our upstanding-looking driver bribed the Indian border guard. In Hindi, he kept on pointing at me and my backpack in the backseat.

Ike's Travels

All three of us were stamped out of India, and we approached the Pakistan border. It was pretty much the same routine as the Indian border, but this time they asked to look in the trunk as well. The driver did this for them, and he bribed the guards also. They had a dog to sniff the truck and my bag, but never opened it. I was sweating and scared shitless.

We were stamped, and I had to buy a visa. They asked me to go inside a building to do this, and it seemed to take a long time. I had convinced the driver and Amar to give me my cell phone, as any traveller had one with them. I told them I had identification on it that may help. They were reluctant to give it to me, but finally allowed it. They warned that I could not attempt to alert anyone.

Amar came into the building to see what was taking so long. The guard advised that I was purchasing my visa and I would be along shortly. Amar looked at me with a deadly look and ran his finger across his throat, and finished by scratching his throat to cover up the sign he sent me.

Just before Amar came in, I had turned my phone on, and it was showing a small amount of battery. I sent Garret a text, "transponder in backpack, kidnapped, help," and deleted the text. I turned the phone off, and when I had my permit, I came back to the car.

Amar and the driver were talking, and Amar asked for my phone. He asked me to open it, and he looked at it, but I think he could not navigate through the menus, put it in his pocket and told the driver to go. We drove for about one hour and entered a garage by a house. I thought this was it, but they took the backpack and me and put me in the back of another jeep with a back deck for passengers like the other ones.

When Garret was relaxing after supper and his phone alerted him that he had a text, he opened it and was surprised to see it was from me, but shocked at its content: "transponder in backpack kidnapped help." He had only heard that we were in Nepal and had no idea where we were or who was kidnapped.

He pondered this for a minute and decided to call his friend on the police force, Suresh. Suresh asked a number of questions and asked Garret to forward the text to him.

He asked Garret about the transponder and whether he knew its identification code. I had provided Garret this information months ago, and he had saved it on his phone and passed it along to Suresh.

Suresh knew the history of my previous arrest and charges and the results of that. He asked Garret where we were, and he told him he thought Nepal, but they may have returned from there.

Suresh linked up with his connection with the secret service of the armed forces in Thailand and asked about any reported kidnapping. They informed him about the disappearance of Richa Shadha, daughter of the movie star Shalha Chadha, in India. There was a ransom demand from the kidnappers with a request for a large sum of money to be delivered to an undisclosed location in New Delhi.

Suresh informed them of Garrett's text and the other history from Thailand and the incident with drugs. Suresh advised the Secret Service of the transponder and its ID code.

Suresh was waiting at his home as he was off shift, and after about one and a half hour, his cell chimed. The transponder locator had been activated by Thailand, Pakistan's and India's secret service, and there was a signal from an isolated area in Pakistan near the border with India near Karian. Suresh was advised it would be monitored and they would update.

The secret service commander, Bashar, with whom Suresh was a good friend, called him and advised that a border crossing incident a few days ago may have something to do with this. They were trying to piece together the puzzle, and he advised that the ransom had been dropped and there was no trace of it. It had disappeared along with a white backpacker who had entered the drop location for the ransom money, a clothing store.

It was an ongoing investigation, and nothing had been determined yet. Garret reminded Suresh that the transponder was sewn into my backpack. Suresh alerted Bashar of this, and Bashar was contacting his senior officer and also trying to link up with the Indian and Pakistani secret services. They often do not cooperate with each other very well, especially with three countries involved.

Garret had decided to take his own action and booked a flight to New Delhi and advised Suresh and Bashar that he would like to be part of any action taken, as he could identify me and anyone with me.

Garret arrived in New Delhi and was contacted by Bashar. There was a team of combat secret service standing by to fly west to the Dhawan Colony near Karian and attempt to locate the transponder, which may locate the backpack, and no one knew what else or who else. There were some high-level discussions that resulted in Bashar being assigned to put together a combat team and fly to the region in a black hawk helicopter.

Garret took a cab to the airport and linked up with Bashar, and a team of five combat-ready commandos, and they departed in a black Hawk helicopter. They arrived at Dhawar Colony airport and refueled, and the information was that the transponder had been stationary but was now moving.

The team departed from Dhawan Colony with their own locator in the helicopter pinpointing the transponder.

It was dark before we left that garage, and we were on back trails and four-wheel drive was required. I knew the end was near. The driver and Amar were passing a bottle between them, and there was much laughing and cheering. Nothing I could do, I would have been killed and thrown in the ditch.

After a couple of hours, we arrived at the same camp when I was first kidnapped. They threw me into the same cave cell, and Richa was there.

Outside in the camp, there was much cheering and obvious celebrating in progress. I told her what I had been made to do, and now I was very worried for our lives. She was crying and hanging onto me.

After some time, she had calmed down and said there was a woman who had arrived in their camp, and she was with the leader. She had heard her trying to convince the leader to let her go once the money was received.

She had come to see her and was assuring Richa that she would be released, but how were we to know? The woman was quite sympathetic and had treated her very well and actually protected her from one of the gang.

I asked her if any of them had done anything to her, but she said no. I was very tired and fell asleep. It was very quiet, and I assumed the celebrating was over, not good news. I had not told Richa about the transponder in my backpack, and that maybe there is a chance that Garret may have used his police contacts to attempt to find me. It would be almost a day since I had sent the text.

I was somewhat happy that they did not just kill me and Richa. Maybe with this success, they were keeping us to do it again??

May 7, Richa was sleeping, and I got up and tried the door; it did not budge. I had seen a piece of metal that was almost like a knife on the ground. I felt around for it, and when I found it, I carefully squeezed it in where the door latch was, and much to my surprise, the door moved.

I was scared that there would be a guard at the door, so I opened it very slowly and carefully not to make any noise. There was no guard at the door. It was very poor light, but I could see well enough to make my way without stumbling on anything. I had an idea of the layout of the camp, and I crept along the wall that separated the cell from the main open area.

There was a fire smoldering in the middle of an open area, and many of the gang were sleeping or passed out. The air reeked of marijuana, and I noticed lines of cocaine on a table. Many of them may be in lala land, and that may work in my favour. There were three jeeps, and I had not noticed the number of men, but it appeared there were about the same number, probably ten.

I crept near as I dared and almost knocked over an AK-47 rifle leaning on the table. There was a pistol nearby on the table, and I took that as well. I crept back to the wall with the AK-47 and pistol.

I wondered how I could manage to escape. I went back to the cell, and Richa was still sounding asleep. I wondered if I could silently bleed 2 of the three jeep tires.

I crept to the jeep I had been brought in, and my backpack was in the back. I took the keys out of the other two jeeps and tossed them into the jungle. I decided not to bleed tires as it was too noisy. One jeep hood was off I carefully and quietly removed the distributor cap, and once away from the main area, I threw it in the jungle also.

So far, so good, and I crept back to the cell. I carefully put my hand over her mouth to prevent any noise and woke Richa and I explained my plan. I had no clue where to go and how much gas was in the jeep, whether it would start, whether anyone would wake up, many variables, but anything better than dying. I knew they would likely hot wire the remaining jeep. I was unable to take the distributor cap off the remaining jeep and knew they would likely hot wire it and pursue us.

I cautioned Richa about being completely quiet as our life depends on that. We made it to the jeep without any hiccup, and there was some noise getting in, but there was no one stirring. The jeep fired in about five seconds of cranking, and I slammed it into gear and took off.

I never looked back, but heard shouting and some gunshots. The trail was bumpy, but I navigated much worse in my life, maybe not as fast, but I managed. The jeep had about three-quarters of a tank of gas.

We travelled about maybe one half mile and we were topping a hill and I stopped and recovered my backpack from the back of the jeep deck, it was empty and I put it in the cab, I checked for the transponder. I shut the vehicle off and listened. I did not hear a jeep but thought I could hear a motorcycle.

I started the jeep and took off again. It was good light now, and I could navigate much better on the road. There were mud holes and steep portions, but nothing I could not handle.

I came to a much steeper section and, near the top, rounded a corner with a sheer drop-off on one side. After rounding the curve, I pulled over and stopped, shut the jeep off and grabbed the AK-47. Back in Canada, I almost bought one from a friend, so I was aware how to use it. I set the gun on single-shot as I only had one banana clip in it.

I ran back almost around the curve and listened, and definitely heard a motorcycle, and it was not far. The steep bank on the upside of the road offered good protection from anyone approaching, so I crouched down behind a big rock and waited.

The motorcycle came screaming up the incline, headed straight for me. I waited till he was about fifty yards away and aiming around the side of the rock; I fired 1 shot at the driver's chest.

They never knew what hit them. The driver and motorcycle flew off the sheer drop with the driver screaming. His passenger was lying on the road and moving. I ran over to him, and he jumped up and was pulling a pistol out of his pants, so I fired one round into his chest, which blasted him over the drop as well. I was listening and thought I heard a vehicle, but could not tell for sure.

I ran back to the jeep, and about halfway there, I saw Richa standing frozen, and she had seen me shoot the motorcycle passenger. I grabbed her arm and raced back to the jeep and told her to get in.

I started up and blasted off again with still no clue where I was going. I continued at a fast but manageable pace to not put us in danger, as the terrain was mountainous and rough. There were various rock slide areas with huge boulders sometimes sitting precariously near the road on the upside.

I stopped at one particular steel hill near the top and turned the jeep off again. This time I definitely heard a vehicle approaching, but quite a ways off. As I was standing there, I looked on the uphill side of the bank, and a boulder was sitting there looking like it might come down anytime.

Being a civil engineer and having seen boulders moved, I know it would be difficult, but maybe with the jeep. I jumped out and found it had a winch, so I jumped back in and spun it around. I put the winch in freewheel mode and ran to the boulder. I circled it twice with the winch cable and fastened the hook, ran back to the jeep, put the winch in winch mode and jumped in.

With the combination of the winch pulling and the jeep in reverse pulling, I dislodged the boulder enough to move it, and all hell broke loose. The boulder and a mass of other rocks and dirt came crashing down on the narrow road, making it impassable. I jumped out to free the winch, but it was hopelessly stuck under the boulder. I got back in the jeep, got some slack in the cable and then blasting backwards in reverse, I snapped the cable. I spun the jeep around and blasted off away, feeling really proud of myself.

I had been shot at before when hunting as a kid, and knew what a bullet going by sounds like. I heard many of them, and some hitting the jeep. I did some left and right manoeuvres and luckily rounded a corner. I kept going for about a half hour, and I needed a pee, so I stopped on a rise. I was standing behind the jeep peeing and listening, not even paying attention or thinking about proper manners with Richa.

When I finished peeing, she was beside the jeep and ran around to me and hugged me fiercely. She was babbling away in Hindi, stopped and was saying thank you, thank you, in both English and Hindi (Shukriya). I then noticed her hand was over her crotch, and it was obvious she had peed herself.

I started laughing almost hysterically, both from the humour of her accident and the relief of being safe, well, maybe temporarily??.

There were some water bottles in the jeep, and we both took one. When we were drinking, I heard a distant sound that I knew right away to be a helicopter.

We were not especially exposed where we were, so I drove on till we were on a ridge and it was quite open. I stopped again and heard the chopper again, and it was getting closer. I made a flag with my t-shirt and the AK-47, but thought better of that and just used the t-shirt.

The chopper was military grade, and it looked like gunners were on each side. I was away from the jeep, and with Richa beside me holding her hand, I was sure they would know we posed no threat to them.

The chopper circled us a couple of times, and I thought I recognized Garret in the doorway. I shouted his name, but I was sure they did not hear me. The chopper had enough room to land in the clearing, and not to my surprise, Garret was the first one out.

He jogged over to us and hugged me and said, So I see you have another traveling companion. We both laughed at that, but Richa did not understand. I introduced her to Garret and told her I would explain. There were five obvious military trained combat guys looking in all directions with sub machine guns at the ready.

Their commander came over. Garret introduced him to me, and he asked me where the transponder is located. I got my backpack out of the jeep and showed him, and then sat down on the ground.

I felt completely exhausted. The commander, Bashar, asked me my name, and particulars about where, when, how, why, etc. He was recording everything, and when done, he shut the recorder off and shook my hand and said, "So, a Canadian cowboy are you?"

I said I owed it all to Garret; he taught me everything, and Garret differed and said he would have wet his pants just like Richa. She did not quite understand, but the whole group did, and the commander went to the chopper and gave her a set of combat pants. She, with great dignity, went to the chopper to change. After all, she was a movie star's daughter; preppy schools, opulent living and being from India she did not understand our humor.

Garret was on his cell phone and told Anong that he would be home late. She knows there is a story to be told, but is very patient. I thought about using his phone and calling Ina, but did not know their whereabouts, and it could wait.

Another military chopper with Pakistan Air Force identification arrived and sat down nearby, and the commanders were having a conference. They asked me to speak with them and tell them all I knew about the kidnapping gang.

After I described all I knew I advised that they just follow this road back the direction I came, find a rock pile on the road, maybe find a motorcycle in the ditch, I had failed to tell them what I did to the two guys on the motorcycle, and they would find the kidnappers camp, if they were still there. The Pakistani helicopter took off down the road, and I had pity on the kidnappers, but not much.

We loaded in the Indian chopper and were returning to India. We refueled in Dhawan Colony, and they fed me and Richa, and we were able to wash up some. Bashar was still questioning me and asked if there was anything I was not telling him, so I described the two men and the motorcycle incident, and I said it was self-defence. Bashar looked at Garret, then at me, and he said, 'What motorcycle guys and smiled.'

We arrived at the New Delhi airport and were met by a huge number of police and a herd of media personnel with cameras running. When we were escorted through the mob, as we entered the building, Shalha Chadha was there to meet us. Mother and daughter ran and embraced for minutes, both crying and babbling away in Hindi.

After Richa kept pointing at me and telling her mother in Hindi what had happened, Shalha came over to me, and I felt embarrassed. She knelt down in front of me, and she was holding both my hands with hers over her head in a showing of respect and thankfulness and praying. I forgot how dedicated she is to all her dozens of Buddha's and her spiritual connection to them and Buddhism.

Media cameras were running, and the questions were being shouted in Hindi from all directions. We were all escorted through the airport, and a large caravan of vehicles took us to the secret service headquarters. It took many hours of answering questions as I did not know the language.

They finally released us, and Shalha insisted that she is in my debt; I must honor her wishes for a few days. We checked into the Jaypee Vasant Continental hotel and booked a two-bedroom suite. I showered, and a meal was cooked in our suite. I ate, was exhausted and went to bed.

On May 8, we were escorted back to the airport and boarded a Learjet and took off for Mumbai. Shalha hugged me so many times, and she would hold both my hands and pray. She told me she was thanking Buddha for the return of her daughter. Richa was fast asleep in minutes after takeoff, and I was not long after.

Through all this activity, Garret had just disappeared. I assumed he went home, likely caught a flight back to Chang Mi to escape the media hordes and any limelight; he hated that kind of attention.

When we landed in Mumbai, we took a limo, and it had to move slowly through the mobs of media. We left Mumbai, and I assumed we were going to her villa in the country.

On arrival at the country villa, there were not as many, but still a mob of media, and they could not enter the estate. I asked Shalha how long she was kidnapping me for, and she burst out laughing at my humour.

That night, I asked Shalha to use a cell phone, and I called Garret. He made it home just fine and was busy with fruit harvesting and management of his orchard. He said Bashar would come by and have him make a statement.

He also said that Ina had called him and asked what the hell was going on. She thought she saw some international news coverage of a kidnapping victim being rescued, and she thought the white guy looked like me. He recommended I call her, and he said good luck and asked if I had taught her to cuss like that.

I called Ina, and she would hardly stop talking, so I could tell her a mini-story about my involvement in this kidnapping rescue. I said yes, I was involved and was going to fly to Stockholm and delay my Middle East trip for another day.

She was silent and, in a crying babble, said she couldn't wait to see me. She asked if I was leaving the next day. I told her a white lie that I was tied up with the authorities. It was difficult to explain because, with the background of knowing Shalha, I wanted to tell her in person.

She was crying and laughing, and we signed off professing our love for each other. She was going to call her parents and explain to them I was coming to Stockholm.

I never had a day in my life even coming close to the events of May 7, and I hope I never will again. I had a large bedroom with my own bath. I had showered and was shaving my stubble, and there was a knock on my door. The maid advised supper would be served.

It was ironic. I had been a little annoyed with living this kind of upper-class society from my time with Ina, Ingrid and Lars, and here I was again doing the same thing with Shalha. Supper was a four-course meal, and there were about maybe thirty guests who all treated me like I was James Bond.

Many spoke good English, and there were so many questions from so many. Shalha asked me to please tell my story. I told her and the guests that I have strict instructions from the Indian authorities that I need to release no information to anyone, especially the media, as the event is an ongoing investigation.

I spoke privately with Richa and asked her if she had the same gag order, and she did, but I knew nothing about her rapid-fire Hindi conversations all night. Richa was often crying, and Shalha took her away from the crowd.

I was exhausted again and asked to be excused and went to bed. Shalha escorted me to my room and presented me with a Buddha. It was about six inches high and gold in color, and I assumed it was just that color of paint. She smiled and told me that it is one of her favorite Buddhas. She had traveled with it a lot, and she apologized that it is not pure gold but gold-plated.

I did not want to accept this gift of her favorite Buddha, but she insisted and told me she would be extremely hurt if I did not accept. She said she has many and will have another replica of this one made for her travelling. She explained that when Richa was kidnapped, she did not have her similar Buddha with her, and the spiritual protection was not there. I must carry this Buddha with me when travelling at all times. It had served its purpose to return her daughter.

What could I say? I accepted, and she was beaming and crying. It was an emotional moment for me also, because in my life, I rarely pay attention to some figurine or religious item for protection. I was thinking of the kidnapping gang, and they would have laughed and smashed a Buddha like this one.

May 9, I slept in, and Shalha came to my room to wake me and told me I could go for a massage and steam at my leisure. Well damn, here I was again, so I had my massage and steam and a breakfast fit for a king and thought, "When in Rome, one must do what the Romans do!!!" After breakfast, Shalha summoned me to a tuxedo fitting in a studio on the main floor.

I was not aware that there was a large ball planned that night with about three hundred guests, and of course, I was being told I was the guest of honor. Shit, would this stuff ever end? An assistant dressed me, and then a makeup artist apparently did wonders with my mug, first shaving my dome, then darkening it like I was tanned and then was given a little more eyebrows, and I thought maybe I would have to wear lipstick for Christ's sake. I looked in a mirror and thought, "Who is that guy in the mirror?"

There was a band, a clown and a five-course meal after which I was instructed to dance with the other guest of honor, Richa. She was decked out in such a beautiful gown, and the media coverage, although chosen and minimal, was still constantly in my face and a nuisance. Few spoke enough English, but either Shalha or Richa interpreted for me.

Then there was a grand announcement, and some government dignitary was up on a podium and gave a speech, all in Hindi, of course, and then I was summoned to the podium by him.

I was presented with, guess what, another Buddha, with an inscription of which, when translated for me, it said, "This Buddha honours you and will watch over you and Buddha thanks you for your help in bringing Richa back to us." I felt like a goof up there, and as they say in California, "That's Hollywood", but here it is, "That's Bollywood".

I was not aware this whole affair was live and a large promotional event to introduce Richa as the next 'Chalha' movie star, following in the footsteps of her mother. I was thinking that Ina would likely see this and wonder at my joke about finding a woman like her in every one of my trips retracing my brother's journey. Boy, was I going to be deep in Swedish shit!!

I was drinking my share of champagne and then switched to rum. Shalha asked me to accompany her friend, who was one of the current Bollywood stars, to a private room for some photos.

What the hell was this about? But it became clear real quick. Once in the room, she went to a table and from her purse took out a little satchel with white powder in it. This was obviously common for her; she made some cocaine lines and proceeded to snort a couple of them and offered me the tube.

She wanted to share some lines of cocaine with me, then likely share something else as she took off her wrap and was hugging and kissing me. I declined everything and later thought, Jesus fuckin

Christ, would it have been nice to see those big hooters? She was not concerned that I did not want to have sex with her. I think she was thinking of plan B.

She looped her arm in mine, and we re-entered the ballroom. She proceeded with cross-eyed as she was from the cocaine, to lead me onto the dance floor and dance like she was in heaven. Dancing was one thing, but she smothered me with those big hooters, and very slyly she was nipping and licking my neck just under my ear. Christ, I had such a woody, I was sure it showed.

I had to get away from this torture, and Shalha rescued me and danced with me. She apologized for Katrina's behaviour; she was told Katrina wanted private photos and did not know she was going to take cocaine.

My mind was flashing to this being a live event, and surely Ina would watch for it, and the Swedish shit pile will be higher. Oh damn. I made it through the rest of the night, dancing with multiple movie stars, and I did enjoy it, but I was just a little out of my element. I felt like Crocodile Dundee. Back in my room, I locked my door and placed a chair under the knob, just like in the movies.

May 10, it seemed like a long time ago that I had parted with Ina, Ingrid and Lars in New Delhi, but it was only six days. I used Shalha's phone the next day, and Ina was fit to be tied. I tried to explain what all the fuss was about, and I was a captive part of it because of my part in helping bring Richa back from the kidnappers.

She was not a happy camper, and I said I am flying out tomorrow early with one stop in Istanbul and arriving about 10 pm their time. I told her she is my one and only woman that I love, and that has not changed. She had to be happy with that regardless of what she saw on the news, which I did not know.

Shalha came to me and gave me her phone. It was my nephew Mickael who lived and worked in Mumbai. He said he heard about a Canadian boy who had rescued Shalha Chadha's daughter.

He said Jesus Christ, Ike, was that you. Guilty as charged, I said. It was a blast, but I do not want to repeat it. Chances are pretty good I will not be so lucky the next time. He said he had time to come to Shalha's villa and visit. I asked if he could come today as I am flying to Stockholm tomorrow.

He said, "What the hell are you going to Stockholm for, I told him he won't believe me, so it is best he comes out if he can.

I called Garret and he was laughing so hard he could not talk, He said, 'Boyo, are you going to be in big shit with Ina?' I asked what was on the news and he gave me a play by play of Katrina that was nibbling on my ear. It looked like you had a woody. I said fuck you and the horse you rode in on, he just kept laughing. I would be facing one pissed off Swedish lady, but it was not my fault.

Most of my belongings, including my phone, money, passport and credit cards, were couriered to Shala's villa. Bashar called me and asked if I received my possessions and updated me on the case against the kidnappers. He said only two survived, the two that had, unfortunately, run off the road with a motorcycle. He said somehow they appeared to have some gunshot wounds, but neither one could provide a clear account of how they ended up over a cliff in a gully. They were air lifted out and lived. He said the report says they shot each other.

Shalha requested a horse ride with me, and we talked for hours about all the events. She is a lovely lady. She has gone through the worst fears a mother can ever imagine. She is used to attention and media and all the glitter and fame from her Bollywood career, but she said this series of events is the most difficult she has ever encountered.

When we arrived back at the stables, my nephew Mike was there and we had a long chat while sipping rum and beers. He was flabbergasted at the events around the kidnapping, and then I said, "There is more."

I told him about the Georgetown and Chang Mi events with the dope and the kidnapping of Ina. So let me get this straight, he said, "First, who the fuck is Ina?" I told him a quick story about Ina and how we met. His first question was how the fuck old Ina is? I said, 32. He said, "Get the fuck out of here. You are bullshitting me. I thought that before when you called me about visiting Su."

I showed him many pictures from my phone of Ina and me together. He said, "You old bastard. About ten times, he was laughing so hard. Only old Uncle Ike can pull off these types of things," he said.

'So, where is Ina now?' He asks. I said, Stockholm. So that is why you are going there? I said yes, 'but my original plan was to follow Les's trip across the Middle East before I got kidnapped. Now I changed my mind.'

He said, 'What are you doing here?' And that's when Shalha came back from her shower, and she hugged Mike and they caught up on some of the events. She told him that Buddha sent Ike after the kidnappers to rescue Richa. I did not differ with her, and she said that most of the ransom money was returned. Then she was smiling and said, "She is giving it all to me."

This surprised me as I had no clue what she was talking about, and I said, 'That will not happen.' She said it already was, and there is nothing I can do about that. I said, "Say what?" You think I will just accept that money. She said, 'Well, you better, or I will send Katrina after you.

Mike was laughing so hard, he asked is Katrina the one that was trying to eat Ike's ear and she looked whacked out on cocaine. Shalha said, 'The very same lady,' and Mike kept laughing.

Now I was intrigued. I was not a rich man, and here was a rich woman about to give me what I considered tainted money. So, out of curiosity, I asked her how much money it was. She looked at me and said, 'Ten million US dollars.' I said, "Get the fuck out of here. You are giving me ten million dollars." She said, "You bet your sweet bald head, buddy. You earned it. My daughter is worth all my money; that is only a little bit of it." OMG, JHC, is all I could say. My nephew said, "She has a point, Uncle, and if you don't want it all, give me a million or two." We all laughed more.

I sat there, too stunned to think straight. Is this lottery winning or what? It did not seem at all right, but who was I to differ with a rich movie star? What the hell would I tell Ina, my kids, my friends, the pope? Christ, my mind was spinning.

Mike was as dumbfounded as I. We have a colorful history together in Canada and Asia, but nothing like the events that I had experienced in a few weeks, never mind the previous two months.

He kept shaking his head, and we were cheering each other, Richa, Shalha, the pope and Jesus Christ himself. Richa came into our little celebration, and she looked still subdued and stressed. Shalha spoke to her in Hindi for some time, and she was pointing at me several times.

Richa came over and knelt in front of me, took my hands in hers, extended them over her head and was praying. I assumed she was as committed to Buddhism as her mother, and she was paying respect to me and Buddha. She was crying, and I held her in my arms for a long minute. She kept saying, "Shukriya" over and over. She left the room with a doctor, and her mother said it is very special for her to thank me as she had; it is part of her recovery that her psychologist recommended.

Mike was sitting there smiling and as amazed as I was; we were both out of our element. We continued to get plastered, and he stayed for supper, and I poured him into a taxi.

He was so funny. Before getting in the taxi, he was bowing in front of me with his hands together and chanting jibberish to me, and I realized that he speaks Hindi, and maybe he is actually taking up Buddhism religion. He wanted to have me visit him in Mumbai, but I told him I had no time.

May 11, Shalha's one servant came to summon me for breakfast and Shalha and Richa were there. Richa looked much better than the previous day. Shalha proceeded to inform me that she had cancelled my flights. I joked and said, "What, must I fight my way out of here?" She was laughing and said no that will not be necessary, you are still flying to Stockholm but on my jet. You must pack. It leaves in one hour. Wow, more uppity class treatment and I had little choice but to appease this very dominant woman.

We said our goodbyes; I hugged both women for a very long time as this was such a special moment for us. Richa could only utter, "Shukriya" over and over, and I told her to take her time; it will all be fine, but I knew her recovery would be much longer than mine.

The limo took me to the airport, no security, and I was off for a much more comfortable flight than I had arranged with normal economy class on a regular airline. I had a steak lunch and as much booze as I liked, but I slept lots.

I called Garret from the airplane and gave him an account of my visit with Shalha and her daughter at the villa. I did not tell him about my windfall from all the ransom money. I was still in shock over those thoughts about that kind of money and what it would do for me.

I was thinking it was too good to be true and would take it all one day at a time. If I received this money and I was not sure of that, I knew Garret was not a rich man, and his mortgage and possibly an orchard manager and staff to run it would be minimal compensation for the help he had provided.

Chapter 11
"A New Home"

May 11, our flight had one stop in Istanbul for refueling, but our flight time was about three hours less than the commercial airline flight times. After landing and deplaning, I entered the air terminal and had to go through customs and buy a visa as well.

I called Ina, and she was confused—I was not due to arrive for three more hours. I said it is a long story and prefer to tell her in person. I added that I could just catch a taxi, but I do not know where to go.

She was quiet and said, "You are joking with me, right?" And I said, "No, I am here in Stockholm and I can't wait to kiss you." She said she will come herself; she is only thirty minutes away. Please wait. I told her I would find the arrivals, and she can pick me up there.

Ina pulled up in the arrivals road lane in her Volvo SUV. She saw me right away, an old guy with a backpack, and she jumped out and ran to me, jumped into my arms and almost bowled me over. She kissed me fiercely and could not stop talking between kisses. I let her run on and a parking attendant was waving at us so we got into her SUV and left.

While driving, she gave rapid descriptions of speaking with Garret and, with difficulty, pried some information from him. She said that I was involved in the kidnapping of the daughter of a movie star from India.

I tried to fill her in bit by bit, and I said maybe it's best that I tell the whole story with Lars and Ingrid present. She thought that was ok, and we arrived at her apartment. I was new to all this as she had mentioned she lived in an apartment, so she parked in an underground parking and we took the elevator up to her flat.

As soon as we were in and closed the door, she attacked me, and we were shedding clothes as fast as we could. She was as energetic as ever, and it was like being in heaven again with her. We lay together, and she grabbed her phone and called her parents. She had forgotten about them, and they were waiting for her to go to the airport.

They were surprised, with me already being here, and I told them that we can all get together, and I will fill them in. We showered, and Ina was happy to soap me all over. She said she missed washing my beautiful body.

We met Lars and Ingrid at their favorite restaurant, the Aifur, a true Scandinavian atmosphere. We all had the rack of lamb and a fruit wine, followed by some of Lars favorite Swedish Rock rum. Ina, Ingrid and Lars were beyond curious for me to tell them my events of the past six days.

We finished our meal, and I requested that we go a little more private in a booth at the back. When we were settled there, I told them the entire story from the time we parted at the airport in New Delhi. I gave them a detailed story of the kidnapping and meeting the other captive, but not including the shooting of the motorcycle driver and passenger. I explained how I contacted Garret and how he helped again and rescued us with the helicopter and combat troops.

I explained that I had ironically met Shalha Chadha and her daughter years ago. I explained that Shalha requested me to visit her villa near Mumbai. I explained her desire to thank me with the villa visit and the media coverage to help promote her daughter's movie career.

I explained that the movie star Katrina requested some private photos, and all she wanted was to snort some cocaine. Ina said that it was not all that it looked like what she wanted. I explained Shalha's Buddhism, and I would show them the Buddha she gave me. I explained her cancelling my commercial flights and sent me here on her private jet.

I explained my change of plans to not travel the Middle East based on Ina's former kidnapping and the kidnapping of Richa and me. I did not include Shalha giving me ten million US dollars.

They were quiet, and I thought they must be thinking I am off my rocker, how can all this happen to a normal redneck Canadian old man who started traveling a portion of his brother's trip?

I told them it was not fair to put myself into more potential very dangerous countries with all the turmoil and corruption going on. I told them that it is not fair to Ina to worry like she has from our former fiasco and then my scary events.

I said I was here as long as Ina, Ingrid and Lars would accept me. Ina was sitting on my lap, and she was crying again. I thought there were still lots of healing for her to endure from her kidnapping. Lars and Ingrid were quiet and finding it hard to fathom my and Ina's experiences in such a short time. They welcomed me home, they hoped I would stay here and cool my travelling heels for a while.

Ingrid suggested that Ina and I need some private time to catch up, and Ina told her we were at her apartment when she almost forgot about them. This brought some laughing, and Lars proposed a welcome home toast.

Back at Ina's apartment, which was in a very nice mid-sized high-rise and was quite comfortable and modern, we settled in bed and just enjoyed the peace and comfort of being together.

Over the next couple of days, my nephew called his mother in Canada and related the events of crazy old Uncle Ike. Margie, called Audrey, Audrey called Chris, Audrey called Norman, Norman called Richard, Audrey called Irene, and many nieces and nephews had found out from talking to their parents, my siblings, so my phone and text messages were nonstop.

My children Nick and Colby called, and even my daughter called; we do not get along well, so that surprised me. My family and friends started calling me Crocodile Dundee and James Bond. I knew I would be telling my story many times over and it would get old hat, so I was considering writing this story.

May 13, at supper at Lars and Ingrid's this one evening, Ingrid presented me with a top-of-the-line laptop computer. She must have read my thoughts because she asked me if I had considered our discussions in Thailand about writing about the trip. I said I did, and many things were on my mind, and I may have forgotten some things, and Ina can fill me in when my memory has blanks.

May 18, Ina and I were in a routine the past few days, which included her being off to work, and I was writing. The computer had a superb spelling and grammar check, but I still messed up some of the formatting. Ingrid sent me an editor and a technical assistant to Ina's apartment for a day to help me get over some writing humps and difficulties. I did take some breaks to exercise or prepare some meals.

Many nights, we were invited out to restaurants or homes of Ina's family and friends, and it was becoming quite a pain to tell my story over and over. One night, Ingrid advised that I should just answer questions with, "Wait for my book, and you can read it all." She asked me how the writing is going, and I said, "I am not sure, I have never written this kind of detail to this extent."

I don't know if I am slow or if it sucks' Ike said. "It is easy to find out, how much have you got done?" Ingrid asked. I said, "Well, about ten chapters and about 46,000 words." She said, "My god, that is very good." She wanted me in her office in a couple of days to meet with my editor, bring your laptop, and we can download it there. I said she can have a flash drive; I save it on the hard drive and a stick. Ingrid said that it will work, and after Kirsten has read it, she will want to see you.

Wow, I felt sort of strange, all these things were so different from my normal life, and I was enjoying everything immensely.

Ina and I had a loving relationship, and our lives seemed so busy and full; we were very happy.

May 21, we were at Ingrid and Lars's home for supper, and Ingrid told me that Kirsten is impressed with my story; she thinks it has tremendous potential and wants to meet with me the following week. She said maybe you will be a rich man, and I just laughed because I had not thought much about the ten million.

The next day, I decided to log in to my RBC account in Canada. I almost shit myself; it said some figure over ten million. I called the bank and asked to speak with the manager. He assured me that yes, there was some issue with the transfer of this large amount, but after some time, it was finally in their hands.

He advised that I need to address what to do with the funds, and he would assign a financial advisor special to me. I thanked him and went to open a beer and had a couple of shots of Lars good Rock rum. I was rich beyond my wildest dreams.

An hour later, Ina arrived home, and she could see the empty beers and the bottle of rum and a glass with another drink. She looked a little confused and maybe a little angry, and asked why I was drinking; I normally do not drink during the day at all. I got up, gave her a big hug and kiss, and I said, "Sit down, honey, I have something to tell you."

She was looking more worried after that, and she sat across from me and said, "Well, spit it out, old man, you are here and you are not kidnapped." We had sometimes joked about our experiences, me to her and her to her therapist.

I said, "Remember the house listing your mother was showing us the other day." She said, "She did not buy it, did she?" I said, "No, but I may buy it for you, if that is the house you want." She looked quite puzzled because she knew I had some money, but we had never really discussed finances much yet. I said I had recently received a gift of ten million, she assumed I was joking, and she said, "You did not kidnap someone, did you, old man?" and we laughed.

I explained that Shalha was quite religious with her Buddhism, and she gave me the Buddha, which is right there, but I never told you about her choice of giving me the exact ransom money amount that was requested for her daughter. What she said was that her daughter is worth more than all her money, and that is only a little of it, and I deserve it. She said, "Stop joking like that, you are drinking and telling me this bullshit, and I don't like it."

I took out my phone, logged into my RBC account and handed it to her. She was speechless, unusual for her, and I said, "I need a financial advisor, do you know a good one?" She was babbling away and jumped on me, and we tumbled over on the couch. She was up and walking around, and she said, "Don't kid me now, I had a great day, and it is not April 1st." I grabbed and carried her into the bedroom and told her she could show me how much she loves me and my money. We were laughing and had a very rambunctious bout of sex.

Later, she called her mother and explained that we had some good news and we would meet tomorrow for supper at the Aifur restaurant.

May 24, my day of writing went slow, my mind kept flashing to my newfound wealth. I had to modify some of the story about my trip here and there, and writing on a computer allows any number of changes, additions or deletions. Ina came home from her work early as she was so excited about breaking this news to her parents.

At the Aifur restaurant, we found a table isolated near the back, and I ordered 2 bottles of their best champagne. Ingrid and Lars arrived, and Ingrid hates secrets and waiting for this news of ours had bothered her all day. I said, "Ina is better to tell you in your native tongue because it will be much faster and she is busting to tell you."

Ina roared into the story, and many times Ingrid had her hand over her mouth, one time almost choking on a drink of champagne. Lars was smiling and guffawing like a bull moose, and when Ina finished, they both looked at me and both in Swedish were calling me a lucky devil. And we had multiple cheers and drinks. We were into the second bottle before we even ordered supper.

Lars was serious for a moment; he took Ina's hand and asked her if this was some kind of joke, and if it was, he was not happy. She assured him it was not a joke, and he was truthful and said, "He thought maybe the news was that Ina was pregnant." Ina said that it will come, but Ike is shooting blanks at the moment, and we would have to improvise.

Lars, ever the slow Swede to get a joke or one of many English slang expressions, asked, "What does shooting blanks mean? I never saw his gun." We were all roaring, laughing, and Ina explained what it meant in Swedish, then Lars almost choked on his champagne.

I said to Ingrid, "We will be able to buy our own house and maybe a more expensive one than the one you showed us." Ingrid said, "Now who is thinking more like us?"

I told them that I will fly to Thailand and clear Garrett's mortgage, and hire an orchard crew to work for him. He deserves it, but will want to refuse any money. I could fool him and ask him if I can reimburse his flights from Chang Mi to New Delhi, and just increase it some, but I do not know how much that was, and I prefer to do this in person.

Lars also the criminal lawyer, asked if this was all legal. I said it is a gift, and Shalha wants it kept a secret. He said, 'Ike, you are good at keeping a secret." Ingrid said, "You guys better get busy with the improvising and make us a grandchild before Ike buggers off on any trip, that Katrina movie star may kidnap him." We all roared at her humour.

It was a jovial night, and Ingrid and Lars were so enthused about my windfall. They thought Ina could make good use of my money and add me as one of her clients. It was clear to me that they did not consider any of that money for Ina as in a marriage; they knew she would have millions of her own in her inheritance.

I know a couple of rich men back in Canada who are going to die, and their families will fight over who gets what. Greed can do that, but Lars and Ingrid were not greedy.

I told them that I wanted to fly back to Canada and take care of my children. They work hard, but with inflation, my daughter and youngest son would never buy a house. I thought I could buy them a house and they would appreciate it. I would not just give them money.

I did not know the timing of doing this, I am concentrating first on Ina and my life together. I think we are making our relationship work. Ina hugged me and said, "He is a good man, I am very happy.

I said, " I am also really concentrating on finishing my story of the trip, and of course, it does not end in India, as I am here and that is a part of it."

Ingrid was concerned that they would be part of the story. I said, "Well, were you not in Thailand, India and Nepal?" I explained that I am not leaving anything out, I joked, I will not tell about their rejuvenated love life, and Ingrid was not enthused with that comment, Lars was just smiling like a cat sitting and purring.

We had a wonderful evening, and when back to Ina's apartment, she took a marijuana joint out of a cabinet and asked if I was interested. I said, "Does a bear shit in the bush?" She laughed, and we smoked the joint on her balcony and hurried back to bed with our enhanced appetites.

The next week, **May 26**, Ingrid set up a meeting for me with my editor, Kersten. She was quite enthused about my progress; she told me that I am not an experienced writer. I am mixing a narrative type of writing with descriptive writing. She thought that my story was based on a quest to follow my brother's journey, but my experiences make it more interesting.

She had my original story I wrote about his journey, and it was very interesting, but a factual history. She said that the story is only short and may be included with the new story of my trip. She said my journey is more interesting, and from her experience, she was interested enough herself to want to read it the same day she got it.

She said it caught her interest, and she is waiting for the rest of it. I told her I was confused about where to stop. She thought about that and said it was approaching the range of most novels, which is between 70 and 100,000 words.

I wondered out loud to Kerstan if I could travel to Thailand to visit Garret, travel back to Sweden, get Ina pregnant, travel to Canada with Ina on a trip and then back to Sweden to continue our life together. Maybe stop there, as it seemed like a likely place. I suggested that maybe I could indicate that more stories are coming with the other legs of my brother's journey, I could take.

Kirsten said, "Well, keep writing and we will see where it takes us." I told her she is part of the story; this confused her, and I said, "Well, I am here, and this is part of my story." She never thought of it that way, but understood my point. She said she would think about it and discuss it with a couple of her colleagues.

That night at Ina's apartment, Ingrid called and asked about my meeting with Kersten. I said, "It seems she thinks it needs to be longer," and I suggested it may include a trip to see Garret, getting Ina pregnant, a trip to Canada to meet my family and end back here living with Ina. I told her she thinks it may include my original story about my brother's trip I already wrote.

She was giggling about the getting Ina pregnant part, she said she is crossing her fingers, toes and eyes that it will happen.

She will meet Kersten and discuss it further with her. She said, "If Kersten thinks it should be published, it will have potential to market, or she would have told you it may not be worth publishing." She values her judgement, and she would not give it a green light if it did not have potential.

Ina was listening to my and Ingrid's conversation and was giving me the thumbs up. She joked that in Thailand, watch out for the movie star; she did not want me kidnapped. She said her therapist was suggesting that humor about our ordeals was recommended, but I'd better not think about seeing that cocaine addict.

Ina had returned to her jujitsu club and was recovering her form and abilities. She invited me to join. I attended a couple of sessions, and the Sensei instructor, Olaf, suggested that I was in terrible shape and that there was lots of work and dedication to even consider taking me on as a student.

He did recommend that one of his junior instructors is where I belong with all the beginners, but I needed lots of work on my physical conditioning first. I started swimming every day, and on some alternate days, took some free weight training with a fitness club. I was challenged by the Sensei, but knew he was right. The trip had not lent itself to lots of exercise or conditioning, unless the sex was considered exercise.

Ina was laughing at the Sensei's analysis of me, and I said, "Wait till you get 75." She compared me to her father, and said he is younger than you and you are in better shape. She said since the trip, he has also joined a fitness club, maybe wanting to trim his physique also.

We had a fulfilling routine to our life, and Ina had mentioned a couple of times that she should make an appointment for us with an in vitro specialist. I was still a little nervous to become a father at 75 years young, but I did not argue with her. I remembered Lars's suggestion, just listen and tell her you love her, as the Swedish woman always gets her way.

June 1, we had an appointment with Dr Hanna Christensen. She explained all the difficulties with extracting sperm from a 74-year-old, considering that I had my tubes tied twenty-five years ago. She said that it is not guaranteed that there will be sufficient sperm, considering the vasectomy and my age.

She asked how active I was sexually, and Ina chimed in that I was very active. This humored Doc Hanna, but she was being straight forward with us, and we should be aware that the chances of success are likely low considering all the facts.

She set up the procedure to extract sperm, which would determine if we proceed to step two. It was scheduled for next week, and I was not looking forward to it, as I did not relish them playing with my knackers.

Whey the day arrived, I came in, and Doc Hanna's team consisted of four females, and they smiled a lot. I think my face was beet red as it felt hot, and I was sedated, and the procedure did not take long. Doc Hanna came into the recovery room smiling and told me there were lots of the little devils, and we can plan the in vitro.

That night, Ina was very happy and excited about the results. She had to monitor when she would next ovulate, and she could become impregnated. The days were numbered and the procedure scheduled. I was not nearly as excited as Ina. I still was flashing ahead to having a baby, which did not bother me; that part I was happy about, but flashing ahead to turning 85 or 90 was a sobering thought, if I made it that long, and Ina would be left on her own.

The day came and we were side by side in an operation room. I thought of Lars's advice, and I said, "I love you, honey." I was sedated, and Ina was not. The procedure took about one hour, and I came around in a recovery room with Ina sitting beside the bed. When I came around, she got up and kissed me and said, "Thank you, honey, I love you."

The next day, my knackers were a little tender. We had our fingers crossed, and hopefully conception date was **June 4, 2026**.

Ingrid and Lars were taking us out for supper the day after the operation. We had a happy time. Ingrid was planning all kinds of things already, and it was premature. The little devils, as Doc Hanna called them, may be slow like me; it sometimes takes more than one attempt, ugggh?

Ina was quite busy at work; she was still catching up from her leave of absence. I continued to write about our trip to complete it, which included our daily lives as we were living them and the possible child we would have if the in vitro worked.

We looked at a number of homes in our price range of about one million Canadian dollars, about seven million Swedish Krona. The experience with having the huge amount of money I had was, at times, very enjoyable, but the way I obtained it still bothered me somewhat.

Ina insisted I buy a car that I deserved, and her friend drove one I had rode in and liked. I chose different and bought a P1800, it was designed like an old Volvo shape from the sixties, but had all the bells and whistles and the current running gear. It is a beast with 430 horsepower, a five-speed standard transmission and dual carburetors. I could not get enough of driving it, but had to watch my speed as it went like a rocket.

"A New Home"

We settled on a house, actually quite near Lars and Ingrid's location. Stockholm is divided, with about half being on the mainland and the other half being on seven islands. They are all interconnected with tunnels and bridges, including the subway system as well. The house we bought was listed at six and one-half million, but I paid much less cash. The realtor was fit to be tied, but I met the owner, and he wanted to buy private and bypass the realtor. The owner let the listing lapse, and that saved me a bundle.

Time flew by with our lives so full and happy, like a fairy tale, and I often thought everything was too good to be true.

I had contacted Garret and told him I was coming to visit, and while near him, visit Shalha Chadha in India as well to thank her personally. I also wanted to get home and reunite with my family and invest in houses for my children.

Ina came home on **July 2,** and she was beaming from ear to ear and jumped into my arms. I had not kept track of the dates, but as a woman, she was counting the days, as I had noticed a calendar in the fridge with days marked off like the twelve days before Christmas. She opened a bottle of champagne by popping the cork with a big yell. She looked at me and rubbed her stomach and said the little devils worked, and we kissed and hugged as we shed clothes and raced into the bedroom. She had refrained from any drinking and smoking marijuana for the entire twenty-eight days and had only had on small glass of champagne.

Jesus Christ, I said, I am pregnant at 75 years young and we lay in bed talking bout this. She called her mother, and there was more screeching and laughing. They wanted us over for supper, and we would celebrate.

Lars and Ingrid had got to know me much better by being here in their home by seeing them much more, and associating with them a lot. Ina and Ingrid were babbling away about redecorating a room in our new house, as we would take possession in about three weeks. They were ecstatic about the prospect of a grandchild.

I called my sister Audrey, because if I gave her the good news, all the relatives would hear about it within a few days. She said, "Dont bullshit me, you old bastard, you are 75 for fucks sake and you are not even married." I told her to mind her language as she was on speaker phone, and we switched to video, and she did watch her language after that. She was going on about how crazy I was, but she said it did not surprise her.

That night back at Ina's apartment, we were so happy and relaxed. I told Ina that I have such mixed feelings about this, but mostly just happy thoughts and anticipation of the pregnancy going good and we have a normal, healthy baby.

"A New Home"

Lars was a great racquetball player, and we met twice weekly at his club. And he usually kicked my ass, but he was younger and had taken his fitness seriously after meeting me, he said. When we went to play the next day, there was an impromptu celebration with the old Canadian guy that many of the club members had got to know from our after-game beers and bullshit sessions.

That evening, when Ina came home, I told her that I had written all I could and was up to date on my story, which included our lives here in Stockholm. I said the house possession was soon, and after that and we had arranged a contractor to handle some minor renovations and moved in, I wanted to settle some things on my mind.

She knew I wanted to make my trip to Thailand to see Garret and then India to see Shalha, and she was all for me making that trip on my own. She said she would rather stay here and settle in our new home and complete the nursery decorating, and make this home our home.

I told her that the title is in her name and it is her home. She was confused and asked what I meant. I explained that it is still our home as long as she will let me stay, but just in her name, and that would be less hassle when I am not here, and a title change would not be required. She was crying about this, saying, I am stupid and I will live a long time, but she knew different, just did not like thinking about it. She was in my arms and led me into the bedroom for a prayer session!!!

July 4, we took possession of our new house, Lars had a friend who contracted renovations, and we arranged for these to be completed. It took two weeks, and I was there many times to set the buggers straight because this was old hat for me.

We moved in on **July 15,** and we were sitting in our living room. Lars and Ingrid were over and Lars mentioned that I knew everything about renovations, and he had been with me when I set the contractor straight a few times and met our schedule. We were toasting the new house, except Ina, who drank water.

Ingrid noticed the gold Buddha on the fireplace mantle. She picked it up and asked me about it, and said it is very heavy. I explained its origin and that it was not solid gold but gold-plated, so don't drop it. She thought it felt like solid gold, but I said no, it is copper with gold plating. I said Shalha was sure of its mystical powers; she had said it brought her daughter back to her, and I said it must be true. I have a fantastic wife with a child in the oven, which brought laughs. I said, "I have great new friends everywhere here from all their friends and family."

Ingrid stood and walked around, and she looked serious, and she said, "Are you two going to be married soon? I want a grandchild with you married, I am old-fashioned." Ina and I had briefly discussed this, but I said, "It really does not matter to me; we love each other and have plans to stay together, but I will agree to whatever Ina wants."

Ina was quiet, stood up and hugged and kissed me and said, "She would like to marry me, would I marry her?" Wow, had I just been proposed to, what could I say but kiss her back and say, "Yes, Dear, I love you." Ina was clinging to me and crying. Lars was laughing really hard as that was his advice.

Ina told them that she already had her wedding gift from me, the house is in her name, which shocked them, but Lars said a wise move in this being Ina's home country and not mine. Ingrid went to the Buddha, and she was standing in front of it, and I assumed she was praying. She turned and asked if I could find her a Buddha.

I said Ina and I had discussed a trip I wanted to take to thank Garret in Thailand in person, and then Shalha in India. I said I am planning that trip soon and would be happy to find a Buddha for her. I told them Ina wants to concentrate on her work, she wants to complete the investment portfolio for me and also get really ahead on all her clients because she will have maternity leave to consider before we know it.

Ingrid's personality had really opened up, and she said, "Do not get kidnapped by the cocaine movie star." We all laughed at this, and Lars said, "Isn't a man entitled to one last fling before the ring is in his nose," and he got a pillow thrown at him by Ingrid.

In the apartment one day, I received a package by courier. Ina was at work. I opened it and found two ring boxes with identical rings with the opal split in half and mounted in each ring. I was saving it for a special occasion, and this seemed like the time. I excused myself and got the two rings I had hidden in my sock drawer.

I said the Buddha must have indicated this occasion for this gift from him. I gave Ina and Ingrid each a little box with the opal rings in them. Ina and Ingrid were speechless, and Ina's fit perfect while Ingrid's was a little tight. They could not stop admiring them. The cousin of Liberties had done a great job. The rings had been mentioned before, but I had forgotten about so it was a nice surprise.

Ina was so healthy and continued her jujitsu workouts, and she advised her instructor had developed a modified program for a pregnant woman. It was more of a stretch program than aggressive jujitsu, and I attended a few sessions. She had an implant installed and a new false tooth for the one I had pulled out in Australia.

We discussed when I should go to Thailand and India, as I wanted to go soon. Ina suggested I take Lars with me, and I asked if she does not trust me. No, she said, but he cannot stop talking about the trip, and you guys can watch each other's backs.

That evening, I e-mailed Garret and asked if he would be home in about a week. The next day, he responded that he would be and asked if the honeymoon was over and if I was a loose goose. Ina laughed at that. I booked for July 20 and emailed my itinerary to Garret. The days flew by quick, and my departure was the next day.

Chapter 12
"Debts to Clear"

July 20, I arrived in Chang MI, Garret picked me up at the airport. He was full of questions about why I was traveling so soon again. I was sure he was thinking of Ina, and I had parted. I explained how things had progressed, and we had a house, and she was pregnant. He said, "Well, you old bastard, how the hell did you do that?" I said, "It was the Buddha that Shalha had given me." We stopped at a bar for some cheers and beers. When we arrived at his orchard, Anong had a feast prepared like always.

We had a pleasant evening catching up on all the happenings since our last meeting. Garret showed me a gold Buddha that Shalha had sent him, thanking him for his help. Garret was describing his poor orchard crops, and he had to let go of all his staff with the poor income.

The next day, Garret was busy in the orchard, and I asked Anong which bank they used, as I had some banking to do. She told me, and I grabbed a tuk-tuk to get to it and asked to see the manager. I told him that I knew Garret Dekoning and I had some business with his property. He was confused, and I explained that I intended to pay off his mortgage.

He was taken aback, and I advised if he would allow me to use his computer and provide me with the mortgage balance. I told him I would have the funds e-transferred and they would arrive today or the next day at the latest. He arranged for me to use another computer for customers, and I arranged an e-transfer for the mortgage balance. I wanted him to call me when the funds arrived and the paperwork was complete.

That night, I called Shalha and advised that I was in Chang Mi and I would like to pay her a visit since I was nearby. I took Garret and Anong out for supper, and we settled in for the night.

The next day, the bank manager called me and advised that all the paperwork was in place and the funds had arrived. I asked Garret and Anong if they would accompany me to the bank, as I had some difficulty there yesterday, and needed both of them there. They were a little confused, but I insisted.

We arrived at the bank and were escorted into the manager's office, and he asked us to be seated. Garret was suspicious as hell and was looking at the manager very angry. The manager asked if Garret and Anong would read and review the documents he handed them. I told him I wanted duplicates of the clear mortgage in separate files and a red ribbon around each.

Garret was pissed and took his ribbon off and was startled to say the least. He said there must be some mistake, and could he bloody explain this as it was not April 1st. The manager just pointed his finger at me and advised that they ask me. Garret looked at me and asked if this was some stupid joke, and I said, "No, you deserve it." They were both totally taken off their guard and laughing and asking how the hell I could do this, and I said it was from a Buddha.

Finally, as per my instructions, the bank manager pulled out a bottle of the best Sansong rum and poured a round of drinks; we all clicked glasses and toasted to their clear mortgage. On the way back to Garrett's place, I advised him that the work crew were back and they had six months of wages in their pocket and he had another six months of wages in his bank account.

Back at the orchard, I properly explained my newfound wealth, and without Garret, I did not know what may have happened to me or Ina. There were many more rounds of Sansong rum and cheers to good times ahead. Anong was speechless for the most part, and she said that Buddha had certainly looked down at them. Garret just scoffed and said, "Bullshit, just good old redneck Get-R-Dun attitude." I toasted that.

July 23, I arrived in Mumbai and I cleared customs and found Shalha's limousine waiting in the arrivals lane outside. I tossed my bag in with me, and he drove to her Mumbai mansion.

Shalha was so glad to see me and said, "Have a massage and change, I have your tuxedo waiting for you." I asked where we were going, and she said to a premier viewing of her daughter's upcoming first film; she said all the Bollywood big shots would be there, so you must be dressed accordingly.

I stopped her and asked her if I could sit down with her for five minutes. She agreed, and I advised her that I had just come from Chang Mi to see Garret, and because of her extravagant gift, I was able to help him out. I told her that Garret and especially Anong are impressed with their Buddha also.

I also said there is more news, and I advised that Ina and I are to marry, and one other small thing, Ina is pregnant. Shalha was so happy for us and would be angry if she were not invited to the wedding. All business in the preparation for her daughter's introduction to becoming a movie star, she said, "Now go get pretty."

I got my monkey suit on, and the event was in a big theater with cocktails and appetizers to start. I had a seat that Shalha pointed out, and I settled in to watch the film. Richa and Shalha and top movie stars, directors and the like were all up front. I was enjoying the film about an up-and-coming movie star's daughter who had been kidnapped and held for ransom. Christ, they had written a script about the true story of what Richa and I had gone through.

I was not surprised, and the guy who played me in that event was much better looking and much younger. I did enjoy it, and as the theater lights were still dark as the movie progressed, I had not noticed someone sitting next to me. I smelled her before I turned to look at her, and I was not surprised that it was Katrina, the movie star I had the unfortunate experience with at Shalha's villa.

She smiled and hugged, and kissed me on my cheek. She looked over the hill, happy; I thought she was likely high on cocaine. Her hand was wandering on my thigh, and I had to stop her; she was bent on a path of no good from my perspective. I begged off to use the washroom, and when I returned, the movie was over. I was concerned that now with the light on and all the media coverage there, sooner or later, Katrina would find me, and I did not want that to get on the news.

The dinner was excellent after and I only caught glimpses of Katrina, and I would disappear as required. There were some photo shoots with me and Shalha, and Richa, but luckily, I managed to avoid Katrina. We made it back to Shalha's house, and I was able to sit down with Shalha and Richa. Richa was happy and I think has recovered mostly from her ordeal, but there would not doubt be therapy for some time yet.

The next day, I asked Shalha if I could find a Buddha for Ina's mother, and she is convinced she needs her own, as she is completely inspired by the one you had given me. She took me to her Buddha artist, and she instructed him to make one identical to mine. He stopped her instructions and brought out a duplicate of hers. He said they have sold off his shelves since the story about her old Buddha had hit the news. She told him about what it had done for me so far, and he was taking notes to have this hit the news also.

My trip was going great, I had seen Garret, seen Shalha and Richa, found a Buddha, and now I would visit my nephew here as well. I called Mike and he said, "Where the hell are you now, uncle?" I told him, and he said, "Well, no surprise you just show up in Mumbai, come on over. I said my goodbyes to Shalha and Richa. Shalha was reminding me to give her notice for the wedding. I took a taxi to Mike's apartment.

Mike was as surprised as the last time that I showed up in Mumbai. We sat around and caught up on all the experiences since I left here a few months ago. He was not surprised at anything I was telling him, he said, "For Christ's sake, Uncle, write a novel about this." I said, "Well, I have already started one and it is well on its way."

I then told him about Ingrid and Lars's publishing company, that they own fifty-one percent shares, and she has an editor assigned to me and is coaching me along. I told him that I expect to cover Ina and my marriage, and a trip back to Canada and end it there.

He stopped me there and said, "Marriage, you rotten old bastard, she is half your age." I just spread my hands and smiled, and he almost shit when I told him she is pregnant. He said, "How the fuck did you do that?" And when I told him, he was laughing so hard. He said, "So let me get this straight, you had sperm sucked out of your nuts and she had them implanted, and she is pregnant, well I'll be fucked." I said, "Yup, the Doc called them little devils." We had a great time and lots of rum and beers.

I had a video call with Ina, and Mike was quite drunk and he told her that Ike is one of the luckiest bastards he has ever known. She agreed with him and told him to watch my ass so the movie star does not kidnap him. After our call, I reminded Mike about Katrina and also about our latest meeting at the movie premiere. Mike, being Mike, said, "Well, you banged her, didn't you?" And I said, "No, I ran the other way, that would have been suicide."

We continued talking well into the night, and like old times, I bunked on the couch at Mike's. The next day, I had a flight booked home to Stockholm. I was very pleased with this trip and managed to visit with Mike as well. When I left, Mike asked me to make sure he was invited to the wedding. I said, "You and Becky, Garret, Anaong, Shalha and Richa maybe can all come on Shalha's jet. "Sounds like a good plan," he said.

Chapter 13
"Home Life in Stockholm"

July 26, I arrived in Stockholm after stops in Saudi Arabia and Frankfurt; I was bushed after a whirlwind trip and glad to be relaxing at home with Ina. We were lying in bed, and I was rubbing her stomach and commenting on how she had become a little bigger even in two weeks. She was so happy to see me and showed me how much she missed me.

The next day at breakfast, Ina commented that I seemed far away with my thoughts. I told her I was really happy with the trip, and she wanted to know all about it. I told her play by play, but left out the part about Katrina at the theater.

I said it was closure for me and such a boost for Garret and Anong, who were in a bit of a pickle with the orchard, but would survive just fine now. I explained how Richa had improved immensely, and with the movie about her kidnapping, her therapist recommended the movie and said it was like a healing therapy for her to relive it and then put it behind her.

I then told Ina I was missing my family, as it had been more than seven months since I left, and I wanted to take her to Canada. I wanted her to meet my family and see Canada and the river beside where I was born. She was confused and asked why beside a river. I tried to recall if I had told her about being born in a car in the Battle River Valley.

She said she did not know that, and when I said, "That is why I have the 36 Chrysler on my right shoulder and the 50 chev on the other shoulder." She was amazed at the depth of my stories in my life and the new ones that keep coming up. That night at diner with Lars and Ingrid, when she told them I was born in a car, Ingrid laughed and said, "She was not surprised, there is lots of hidden stuff we must pry out of the old man."

She asked, "If I were ever in prison?" Lars guffawed at that and said, "Ingrid, for Christ's sakes, that's not funny." I replied that I was in jail in New Zealand 2 nights with Ina in the same cell and enjoyed it immensely, and other than that only spent 9 years of a 15-year sentence for manslaughter. There was dead silence with that remark, as they had come to realize that there was a long history of my life they knew nothing about. I let them stew about that for a minute and said, "Gotchya, that part is not true." Ingrid threw a pillow at me, and Ina tackled me and sat on me.

I told them that I wanted Ingrid, Lars and Ina to come to Canada to meet my family, what was left of it. I said I wanted them to meet the remaining siblings. I also told them that I wanted to arrange a large gathering for all of my family's nieces, nephews, my uncles and aunts. I could get my sister to arrange this with everyone; I would fly them all to a central, picked location, book an entire hotel and have a weeklong party. I said, "What is the money for if I cannot enjoy my family with my newfound family?"

Ingrid was silent, and then she said, "She thinks that is a great idea and would consider maybe flying all her family to Canada for this gathering." Ina was surprised that Ingrid would consider this, as she is normally tight with her money. Ingrid explained that the company is doing very well, and she needs some expenses to write off, which would qualify. "Her accountant would find a way, if not, what the hell?" She said, "We cannot take it to our grave."

Wow, with this simple suggestion, all of a sudden, we had a party in the making for about 100-200 guests, I thought. We thought about this idea some more and discussed that a suggested date for this should be in the future sufficient enough, as it would take a long time to make all the arrangements, and all the invited guests would need to somehow take time off from their jobs and lives.

I said that besides family, I am sure Garret, Anong, Shalha and Richa would love to go on an adventure to Canada on her jet. There were lots of ideas in mind, and Ingrid said, "She had just contacted the travel agent, her sister and plan everything from her end." It was an idea that took shape quick, and I thought would grow just like cancer, and I really wanted this to happen.

That night, Ina and I were lying in bed and talking about so many things. She said, "She wonders if my family would like her?" I told her that they would all think Ike is the luckiest man on earth. She showed me how much she liked me as we had a prayer session.

The next day, I was on the phone with my sister Audrey and told her my idea. She was silent and then said, "And where the hell do you think to have this high fallutin affair and who the hell is going to pay for it all?" I told her that in Thailand and India, I had robbed two banks, and they are still looking for the bastard. She was silent because, from what she had learned and heard from me in the last year, she was not sure about this statement.

She was still silent, so I told her I had not robbed two banks, but I was thinking of how to manage the costs and not give away my estate value now. She said, "How the hell do I think everyone will pay to come to this affair and be there for a week?" I told her it was just an idea for now, and I would discuss details when I come back to Canada soon.

When Ina came home, I explained that I had called my sister, and she said her mother had called her a few times at work and had already talked to her sister to start making a list of all her family. The idea was blooming and in progress in one day.

That evening, we had Ingrid and Lars over, and Ingrid and Ina were chatting a mile a minute. I explained about my conversations with my sister and brother, and they would think about this possible planned gathering.

Ingrid explained that she knows I have some money, but she wants to cover half of my cost if we rent a resort and cover all her family's travel plans. She was halfway into making this idea a reality. I suggested that it was her choice and would not complain about that. She said that she and Lars have broken out of their boring life, that she did not think was boring till they met me. Lars was just smiling and said, "Yes, honey, I love you."

I had settled into routines of sorts. Ina kept working, and I kept writing. I met with my editor every time I needed to update her on progress, and the novel was nearing completion. I had thought about how it would end. The obvious choice to me was after I returned to Canada and settled my affairs there with my children and caught up with everyone.

I found that I still had lots of energy, but after the travel, I was tired for weeks. I was 75 years old, and two known facts about our life are taxes and death. After a racquetball game with Lars, my knees would hurt for days. The body can only sustain the level of activity that one has in their youth for so long; the body wears out, some slower than others. I think mine was lasting good, but I was accepting my limits as they were inevitable.

I was so happy with the new Volvo sports car I had bought. I took Ina out for many rides, but after the first one, where I showed her just how quick this beast can go from zero to 275-300, she almost had a heart attack when she realized what our speed was. She yelped, "Slow down, please." After that, I drove more or less the speed limit. The car was a beast.

Weekends, we toured the northern parts of Sweden and much of Norway. The rides through much of both countries are very picturesque. The roads are really well designed and built to standards that travel at speeds beyond the speed limit is not really dangerous, but try to tell that to Ina. I heard "Slow down" lots.

Ina was a little tentative driving the Volvo. After a few trips, she was starting to get used to the car's incredible power and handling abilities. I found I was putting my right hand to the ceiling chicken handle and hanging on. She surprised herself when putting the car through its paces on mountain curves. Her smile and that exhilarating look one gets when a car is being pushed to near its limits are great to watch.

These little weekend trips were such a pleasure; the people were always so friendly, the service was top-notch, the food was great, and there was rarely ever a thought of your life being in danger. We both shared thoughts about our VW van in Australia and how wonderful that trip was. The only downside to the weekend trips was the high costs, as I was still not used to having an almost endless supply of money.

Being as far north as Sweden and Norway are, the fall and upcoming cold months are similar to the Canadian climate at this time of year. I found the Stockholm humidity made the cold chilling to the bone. I was itching for some adventure, and deep-sea fishing was always on my mind. I checked out some charter companies in Stockholm and asked Ina, Lars and Ingrid if they were interested. Lars and Ina were interested, but Ingrid thought we would freeze or drown.

I booked a one-day salmon guided trip for four, and Ingrid, although reluctant, agreed to give it a try. **Aug 5** was our booked date. I did not have to explain to these folks how to dress; they lived here all their lives. Lars had fished in his life, but Ingrid and Ina had never caught a fish before.

"Home Life in Stockholm"

At 6 am, we put on the provided floatation suits and we cast off on a 32-foot ocean-going fishing boat with a heated main deck cabin and a lounge below to eat or sleep. The back deck was open where the fishing took place. We travelled about thirty minutes into the Baltic Sea, the guide was locating his favorite spots with a GPS and fish finder to see the fish volume when we arrived at these locations.

The first location we bottom fished for ling cod while sitting more or less still, and the excitement that Lars and Ina showed and their ability to reel and pull in a fish, was great to see. We caught near our limit of ling cod, and Ingrid still had not handled a rod. She was enjoying the newfound excitement both Lars and Ina were showing, and I thought it was only a matter of time till she tried.

At our next location, the guide set up the downrigging gear, and we were now trolling for salmon. He was using similar rigging that I have used and found good luck with in Canada off our west coast. The guide realized that I was able to help him out and grab a rod and set a fish, and hand it off to Ina or Lars to fight the fish and reel it in. I coached them not to horse the fish and set their line tensions according to how the fish was fighting, and let it run when it wanted. They soon learned to play the fish out before attempting to land it.

We had hooked a couple of salmon, and even though the fish finder showed some decent volume and some big fish, they were not biting very well. I asked the guide if he had any smelt and he did. I showed him how to cut the head off at an angle and put two hooks into the smelt, and how the resulting activity when trolling imitates a small fish swimming. After that, we had trouble keeping fish off the lines and often had double headers.

Ingrid was so caught up in watching and was often beside Lars when he was fighting a fish. One rod dipped right down to the water, and I knew a decent fish had hit the bait. I grabbed the rod, set the fish and then handed it to Ingrid as she was handy and Lars and Ina were not. She was a little tentative, and I told her just to do what Lars had been doing, and I stayed by her side to ensure that she did not let the rod go.

She was doing very well, but it was obviously a bigger fish, and she was having real trouble reeling it in. She asked me to take the rod, and I fought this puppy for about thirty minutes, and the guide netted it for me, and it was a forty-two-pound lunker.

Everyone was quite thrilled with the new experience, and it was noon, so we steamed closer to the mainland and we anchored beside a little Island. The charter company had a little cabin there and a nice fish filleting bench, and a cooking area beside the cabin.

I showed them my fish filleting abilities, put corn meal and lemon pepper shake and bake on these fresh fillets and cooked them up in lots of butter. We had fresh-cut onion rings and French fries along with a nice cold slaw, and Lars, Ina and Ingrid ate their fill and were really enjoying the experience. They said I should buy my own boat because I don't need anyone's help.

After our lunch, we were lounging in the cabin enjoying some of Lars's good rum, and the guide gave us an hour, and then we headed back out to finish our fishing. We caught a few red snappers and some sea bass at the guide's favorite spots for these. We only fished for about another hour and were steaming back to the main dock.

On the way back, the second mate on the boat was filleting all our fish, and he was amazed at the speed I did mine compared to his. I explained to Ina, Lars and Ingrid that they wash up all the fish, vacuum wrap the fillets and quick freeze them. I requested the big one, which Ingrid and I had caught, to just have it gutted and only keep it refrigerated.

Lars, Ina and Ingrid were talking steady about this fish or that fish and how much fun they had and learned. I told them we would have about twenty kilos of froze fillets that we can enjoy. The forty-two-pound salmon, I suggested we invite a gang of family over, and I would cook that up for a feast.

That evening, Ina and I were lounging on the couch, worn out from the day of fishing. She was so relaxed, and it was at times like these that I would realize she was feeding two, and it also took more energy as she was fast asleep in my arms.

Ina would show me the progress of my investment fund and the taxes that it was subject to. She was wondering if there was any business that I may be interested in starting for write-off purposes. She advised that I do not have to operate the business, just hire others for this, similar to what her mother does.

I thought about this and told her that if I had my choice, I would buy a small ranch in Canada. I could hire the ranch manager and hands to operate it and just oversee it. She was intrigued by this idea, as it would be all new to her, but it was part of my life as a youth. I agreed and said, "It was always my dream to have a small cattle ranch."

She asked what kind of price this small ranch would be. I said that, of course depends on many things, but with the location I had in mind in the Okanagan valley, I would assume about one and a half million Canadian may be enough. She would review my portfolio and advise me on what may be the best solution.

Aug 8, we had a BBQ for the big salmon. Ingrid was worried about how many it would feed, and I said about twenty-five, but a good idea to have some chicken wings also to make sure there was enough. She was curious if I had done this big a fish before, and I said, "Does a bear shit in the bush?" She was frowning till she got the comment and laughed. She said, "I guess I should not doubt you."

I stuffed the salmon with onions and lots of garlic, lots of lemon pepper seasoning, butter and some chilli pepper flakes, and then lots of butter around the outside and more onions, garlic and seasoning. I had it triple wrapped in tinfoil and cooked it for about one hour on a BBQ on high heat. When I unwrapped it and took the skin off and pulled out the backbone, there was plenty for all twenty-five at the meal.

Most at the meal had not had fresh salmon like that before, and there were many comments and praises. The meal was a great feast, and Ingrid gave me a big hug and was so impressed at my knowledge and experience. Ingrid is great at putting together a meal of this size, but she really appreciated the help.

The ranch idea was filling my mind, and I was searching on the internet and had contacted a real estate agent my brother knew in Kelowna. He was searching for me and had a number of properties in mind. You cannot buy something of this nature without looking at it, so I was waiting for the advice from Ina about what funds would be wisest to use.

One evening, Ina told me that I could spend two million on a ranch and still have sufficient funds in my portfolio to sustain its amount or likely grow. Holy shit, that excited me big time. I told her I had been searching on the internet and also had a realtor looking. I wanted to go look at many properties that suited my criteria. I also wanted to look into buying homes for my children.

Ina and I were discussing the necessary trip to Canada. I was interested to look at houses for my children and the cattle ranch for myself, but I also wanted to introduce Ina to my family. She was very busy at her job, but I suggested that she could come over for a week or ten days and then come back by herself. I could stay to complete the purchases I wanted to make. I did not tell her, but I may be able to do a little hunting as well.

We booked for **Aug 13**, and I called my sister Audrey and asked if she would let everyone know I was coming home for a visit with Ina. It was a rush for Ina to make all necessary arrangements for all her clients, but with the internet, she could do some work while we were on the trip anyway.

Chapter 14

"Ina meets My Family"

Ina and I arrived in Edmonton after one stop in Toronto. I rented a SUV and we started our first visit right next to the airport at my brother Norm's home in Leduc. He had arranged for his two boys and their families to be there. Ina was charming as she always is, and we had a great first visit.

We had supper there, and I had booked a room in Leduc for the night. The next day, we traveled to Ponoka and picked up my sister Irene, and traveled together to Bashaw to visit my oldest brother Richard in the seniors' home where he lives. My niece Tammy and her family live close to Bashaw, so we had supper at her home.

She is so inquisitive, and she commented that Audrey had suggested I had robbed two banks in India, to which I replied, "When you are traveling, sometimes opportunity arises and sometimes bad things happen." I was not describing my newfound wealth to anyone.

After supper at Tammy's home, we travelled back to Ponoka, dropped Irene off at her seniors apartment, and went to stay at my nephew Dwayne and Donna's home for the night.

The next day, we traveled back to Edmonton and met with my daughter, Kim, and my son Colby. We took them out for supper, and my daughter was like she normally is with me, very opinionated and almost angry. I had warned Ina that she could be quite contrary with me, and that was the case. Kim was asking Ina all kinds of questions about us, and Ina was patient, though I could tell she was disappointed with Kim.

Colby was very charmed with Ina; they talked freely with each other, and this also pissed Kim off. It was not a great visit, and I left my trip history, my new wealth, and my plans to purchase a home for each of them until after Ina had returned to Sweden.

We stayed at the West Edmonton Mall Hotel that night and were up early the next day, and traveled to Valmont to my son Nick's home. We stopped in Jasper along the way, and Ina was impressed by the Rocky Mountains. When we drove by Mount Robson, the tallest peak in North America, we were lucky that the weather cooperated, and it was as clear and the mountain as domineering and beautiful as ever.

I get along best with Nick out of my three children, and he recently moved into his shop-and-home combination. I booked a room in Valemont and Nick had prepared a moose roast in a slow cooker. After supper, Ina was tired and she went to sleep on his couch.

Nick and I went for a walk, and I told him that I wanted to describe my trip, but that he should just listen and let me finish the whole tale first. I told him the whole series of events from when I left Vancouver till today. He did not interrupt, and when I was done, he was flabbergasted and asked many questions, including, "So you tell me you got ten million?" I opened my RBC bank account and showed him what was in there. I told him the other seven million was being managed by Ina; she manages investment for many clients, a few with my kind of volume, but some with even more.

I told him what I planned to do for him, Kim, and Colby, and that I might buy a cattle ranch near Kelowna for myself and Ina. After meeting the real thing, Ina, he had little choice but to believe me, though I could tell his mind was in turmoil. I also told him about my plan to write a book about the entire story I had briefly described to him, and that Ina's mother has a publishing company and one of her editors is helping me write it and eventually publish it. I told him her parents have hundreds of millions and are truly salt-of-the-earth people.

He was getting a clear picture of my fairy tale story and I said "Hey, I never expected to meet Ina, I certainly did not expect to have her want me long term, I did not expect either kidnapping and most certainly was absolutely astonished at the gift of ten million and did not expect to get her pregnant." I said, "I am the luckiest man on earth, and I pinch myself once in a while thinking this is not real, but here Ina and I are."

He looked at me and said, "Hold on, you're saying she is pregnant? So that's why she is tired and starting to get that little belly. You old bastard." Then he asked how the hell we did that, and when I told him, he just shook his head and was blabbering. I said, "Well, none of my kids are giving me grandchildren, so I decided to do it myself." He was laughing very hard and hugged me while lifting me in the air and squeezing me.

I told him that he is the only one who knows of my good fortune, and I want him to keep it to himself. Everyone else can read it in my book, and I don't care who believes it or not.

Ina was awake when we returned from our walk, and she could tell we had been talking about us. Nick hugged Ina, and I could tell that they would get along very well. He told her that I had spun a tale that most people would never believe. She said, "Most of the time we cannot believe it ourselves." We talked till late, and Ina was tired again, and we went back to our hotel.

"Ina meets My Family"

Aug 16, we left Valmont early and drove to Kamloops and carried on the route going to Vancouver through the Hell's Gate Canyon along the Fraser River. Ina was in awe at the scenery, the water volume, and how spectacular Hell's Gate was. We stopped at Hope and got a room in a motel, and visited my brother Tex's daughter. Ina was really enjoying BC and all the stops to visit.

The next day we arrived at Vancouver and visited my sister-in-law Margie, and toured around some. We stayed in the Sylvia Hotel near English Bay and Stanley Park.

Aug 17, we travelled east from Vancouver to Peachland to my brother Chris's home. Chris and Brenda are the worldliest people I know. They have traveled extensively, and when we arrived, he was a little reserved. I thought he was wondering who the hell I had with me and what the truth about my trip was.

They had a fantastic supper all prepared, and he opened some of his best wine. After supper, Chris wanted to go for a walk with me. Brenda and Ina were soul mates right off the get-go, so we left them talking. Chris asked me to "Spill the beans, Ike, and don't bullshit me."

As Chris is like my son Nick, I could tell him the whole story. I described the entire trip much as I did with Nick. He was constantly looking at me in disbelief, but after showing him my RBC balance and telling him Ina is managing the rest, and saying

250

"No bullshit, Chris, just good luck, and I am the luckiest man on earth, and Ina is proof of that," I believe he was starting to believe me.

Back at Chris's home, Brenda and Ina were still deep in conversation, and I could tell they were on the same page. Brenda got up, came and hugged me, and told me that I was the luckiest man she knew. Chris said to Brenda, "You don't know the half of it." We talked late, and I told Chris that Ina is flying home in a few days, and I would be back.

Aug 18, we left Chris and Brenda's home and drove to Casalgar to visit my sister Audrey. Audrey was similar to Chris in that I could tell she was thinking, "What is wrong with this picture Ike had told everyone, and who is this Ina? Audrey had a supper planned and was firing off questions at a rapid pace. Some were directed at Ina, and she answered with patience and elegance. I could tell Audrey was still thinking that there was something wrong with the whole story, but just could not twist her head around what we were telling her.

Audrey, being a nurse, commented to Ina, "I know you are pregnant and I would say about 5 months." Ina laughed and said, "That is close, I'm due in March."

Audrey was getting more comfortable with Ina after our supper, and we left for our hotel because Ina was tired.

"Ina meets My Family"

The next day, we drove to Calgary and stayed in the Fairmont Palliser Hotel. I invited my friends Jim, Kelly, Mike, and Shelly to join us for supper. They were very curious about Ina and me, as they knew nothing about our trip or experiences, and I told them very little. I think Jim and Mike even thought I was traveling with a hooker.

The ladies went to the powder room and seemed to be gone a long time. Mike and Jim were asking questions about Ina, but I was being evasive with my answers. When they returned, Shelly and Kelly asked me to tell them more about Ina and my trip. I said that it would ruin my book, I am writing about that, and they would have to wait till it is finished.

I know Mike was very sceptical about the true story, but was biting his tongue. Jim was laughing his head off as he thought there was something funny going on, but he was finding the humor in its intrigue and secrecy. All I said was, "I am the luckiest man on earth." Mike's comment was that maybe Ina is the unluckiest woman on earth. Ina's response was to sit on my lap and kiss me. She looked at Mike and said, "He is all mine, and I am the lucky one."

They left us, and Mike was surprised when I paid the bill. I said, "Ina is loaded." I think they will be talking about "the rest of the story" till sometime in the future, when I set them straight.

We had a great night's rest at the Fairmont, and we slept in late. I ordered a massage for both of us, and we finally got away at noon and were in Edmonton on **Aug 22**. On the way from Calgary, we made a detour at Lacombe and drove to our old farm location, and toured for around an hour. We then travelled up Highway 21, and I showed Ina where I was born in the '36 Chrysler.

I booked a room downtown at the Hotel MacDonald and invited my best friend Mert, Rena, Barry, and Liberty, the friends from the Philippine house, to supper at the hotel. At supper, there were more questions from Mert and Rena about Ina. Barry and Liberty listened to the questions and then told Mert and Rena about our visit to their home in the Philippines. I think that satisfied Mert and Rena that Ina was real and not something else, like a hooker?

Rena, the ever outspoken African American woman, commented that they had met women from China and another from Brazil who had visited me. She said she is not surprised that I have another visitor. Ina was laughing about this and not at all concerned or upset. She said to Rena, "He has promised me that I am his last and only woman, we are going to marry and have our child," as she patted her stomach. Rena, a long-time nurse, said, "I knew it and asked Ina if she was about four months pregnant." Ina said, "Close," and we all had a good laugh at that. My long-time friend Mert ordered the best whiskey, and we toasted this news.

Later in our room, Ina was curious about the women from China and Brazil, so I explained about them, and she was amused. She commented, "I am going to keep her, aren't I?" I said, "Yes, dear, I love you very much and you are forever." She showed me how much she liked that answer.

The whirlwind trip was tiring for Ina. We slept in the next day and booked massages and just lay around. Ina had a flight out the next day, **Aug 26,** to return to Sweden. That evening, I invited Joanne and her boys, Dan and Jack, and Jack's fiancée, Chrissie, out to the hotel for supper. Ina knew that Les was gone, but he was instrumental in our meeting because of my retracing his trip. She told Joanne as much, and it was likely our most enjoyable meal with people who had never met Ina, but accepted her right away. Jack and Dan could not get their eyes off of Ina and were flirting with her.

The night was difficult for Ina and me; we had not been apart for some time and had solidified many things in our lives. Ina was so glad we had made the trip to introduce her to many of my family and see parts of Canada. She was not happy that she would be without me for a couple of weeks and showed me just how much she was going to miss me.

I took her to the airport the next day, and she was crying and told me not to get into any trouble or get kidnapped, our standard warning when parting. I rubbed her stomach and knew that it would be bigger when I returned to our home.

My first task was to approach my daughter and try to patch up our difficult relationship. We are both pig-headed at times, and we needed to find a way past this needless annoyance. I spent the day with a realtor and explained my wishes to purchase two homes. I was not sure of the location of either home, but I did get an idea of the prices and the market conditions.

I met Kim after she finished her work, and we were cordial, but our attitudes were still strained. I explained that I wanted to buy her a house. This surprised her very much, and I explained the background of how I would be able to do this. She was speechless and likely thinking I was full of shit. Finally, after asking many questions, she seemed to accept that I was not bullshitting and it was going to happen.

I asked her to decide where she would want to live, and I said that it could include BC somewhere. I told her that it did not have to be immediate, so give it some thought. We went out for supper, and she never stopped asking questions. She was concerned about the residual effects from the kidnappings, but I assured her that I was fine.

I could not answer every detail and explained that she will get a first edition of my novel, which I was writing about the trip, including this chapter about Ina and my trip here. She was very surprised at this news and was very interested and looking forward to reading it.

I left her with a much better feeling about the progress we would make in the future with our friendship.

I still had a room at the Hotel MacDonald, and I relaxed and made a few phone calls. I made some arrangements, with my son Colby and my ex-wife for tomorrow, my son Nick in Valmont the next day, and a realtor in Kelowna the day after that. I was lying in bed, and Ina called and she was apologizing that she had forgotten my birthday. I was not in the least upset, as many of my birthdays had gone by this way. We chatted for an hour, she told me that she had visited her parents, and after she had told them all about our whirlwind trip, they were very enthused to plan this Canada trip for their whole Lindgren family. One step at a time was my attitude about this trip, "Do not book flights," I said, and there is much planning required.

I went for a visit with my son and my ex-wife, where he lives. It went like many of these visits, in which I revealed my status with regard to my wealth and my plans for Colby to have his own house. Diane was quiet, and I assured her this was all true, and Colby can attest to Ina being real, and she already knew that, as he had described our first visit with him and Kim.

I left them with all this on their minds, and they should decide on a location for a house for Colby, and the price range I told them was about half a million. Diane was totally in shock about everything and hugged me and wished me luck with Ina. She said Colby thought Ina was pregnant, and I told her about our tasks to get that accomplished, and she was really laughing at this as she said, "I was responsible for you getting a vasectomy in the first place."

There are always stories about an ex-wife wanting more money in cases where the ex-husband came into money, but we were divorced, and there was no way she was entitled to any additional settlement, and she was not the type of woman to do this anyway. She wished me a happy birthday, and Colby was sorry he had forgotten about my birthday. I left my son Colby and my ex-wife with a good feeling about that visit.

Chapter 15

"Elk Hunt"

I had time to travel to Valmont and arrived there on
September 5. Nick was quite busy as he is still building his shop-
home, and his plumbing, heating, and sewer business is
flourishing. I asked him what he was doing from Sept 9 to 15, as I
would like him to take the time off, if possible. I explained that I
had contacted a guide and outfitter in the Fort Nelson, BC area
who had a four-man hunt canceled and could fit me in.

This was all really impromptu, because it was only yesterday
that I had come up with this idea, and luckily, there was an
opening in the outfitter's busy scheduled hunts. Nick was hesitant,
but he said he could make some calls and try to reschedule jobs.
An hour later, he arrived back at his home, and there was a gleam
in his eye; he could manage the time off.

When he was gone, I had called Ina and explained my plans
for this elk hunt. She was worried about my safety, but knew all
my experience with hunting most of my life. This was a safe,
arranged hunt, and she wished me good luck.

I had also called my good friend Bob Johnson from Penticton, and we caught up on some things, and I asked what he was doing and if he was interested in a fly-in guided elk hunt on Sept 9 to 15. There was a cancelation, and room for four hunters, and he would be the third. He was hesitant, and I told him the cost was my treat, which convinced him. He agreed in the next few minutes and said he would settle some things he had to do and be there in a day.

Then I got to thinking, if Lars had the time or could make the time, was able to scramble and get away from Sweden, what an introduction for him to come for this hunt. I called him and discussed the offer, and he was flabbergasted. He knew nothing about hunting; he had no gun, yada, yada. I told him that he could take this unexpected opportunity, and in the future, we could do this, but this had just popped up with a phone call.

Lars called back in an hour and was willing to come. He would book flights to Edmonton and send me his itinerary. I told him to book flights either to Edmonton or Vancouver, and then on to Fort Nelson, and that would save me some travel if I had to pick him up in Edmonton.

Nick and I had to scramble and prepare our gear and practice shooting our rifles a little. Nick's friend Marty would look after Nick's place and the two cats. By the end of the next day, we were packed and ready and sat down to a moose stew supper. Marty was full of questions about the hunt. Bob arrived in the evening, and we had a great time catching up.

Sept 7, we drove to Fort Nelson. We were all excited for this impromptu elk hunt and had a few cheers to celebrate. We booked a hotel room and the next day picked up Lars from the airport. His connecting flights worked out ok, but he had to overnight in Vancouver before his flight to Fort Nelson. We all sat in a lounge getting acquainted and bullsihitting about the hunt.

The next morning, we were at the Fort Nelson airport, stowed all our gear into a Twin Otter plane along with some food and gear for the outfitter, and were off into the wild. Bob and I had done this kind of hunt before, but totally on our own, so this guided outfitter hunt was an absolute, unexpected pleasure.

We arrived at the outfitters camp, **Sept 8**, the dirt strip was not long, but a twin otter can land almost anywhere with tundra tires. The outfitter was there to meet us, and we packed all our gear and settled into our rooms in the bunkhouse for hunters.

It had all the amenities of a home. His camp had power and heat with propane, but the bunkhouse had a wood stove as well. The main cabin was really set up well, and we had a tenderloin steak supper. The outfitter advised that we were in luck, the food was to be first class, as the hunters who had canceled had special menu requests, and that included lots of goodies he described.

260

Lars was as happy as a pig in shit. He could not believe everything he was experiencing, and I told him this is only the beginning, the real excitement is when the elk are screaming at you and grizzlies are roaming the area looking for meat.

Lars did not surprise me when he brought out a bottle of his expensive rum and shared it with everyone. The outfitter was chucking and brought out a bottle of rum that the canceled hunter had requested. It was top-of-the-line stuff, and the rum was flowing.

There were two hunters per guide, and Lars came with me and our guide, Eddie, an Aboriginal who looked like a bum, but I knew he was here because of his knowledge and abilities. Eddie was questioning me about my and Lars experiences with hunting.

I explained I had many years, but Lars was a virgin. Eddie looked my 7mm Remington over and commented that this looks like a rifle with experience, and with what Lars is going to shoot? I explained that he will observe, and maybe tomorrow I will have him shoot, if he feels like he wants to. Eddie could see I was experienced with someone new.

Lars had never been on a horse in his life, so I showed him how to mount up and explained some things to do, but I would be right beside him always. Edie could see I had horse handling and riding experience as I tightened each horse's saddle cinch strap by kneeing the horse in the gut.

Sept 9, Eddie commented that it was late, and the next morning, he expected us to be outbound at six am. We rode for about an hour, with Lars getting along with riding his horse ok. Eddie had stopped a couple of times and was elk cow calling and listening. He was checking for elk sign, ground scraps, and demolished willow bushes, and any elk dung.

He knew his territory and was excited when, after one stop and some cow calling, he got an answer from a bull elk bugle. Lars eyes were bugging out as he asked what that was, so I told him that was a male elk answering the cow calls. Eddie told us to dismount, and we tied up the horses and carried on walking.

Eddie was checking the wind and cow calling, and the bull was screaming at us and getting closer. Eddie whispered that it sounded like a young bull, and we would likely not want him. Lars was bumping into my back as I think he was a little scared, having never experienced this before. When we finally saw the elk about 200 yards off, I whispered to Eddie that it was a six by seven and was bigger than anything I had ever taken.

Eddie whispered that he had not seen the seventh point on the one side, and I could take him if I chose. Christ, since I have been hunting for 60+ years, I knew that a bird in the hand is better than five in the bush. The elk had gone quiet, but the wind was in our favor. I knew he was circling us to get downwind. Eddie seemed annoyed when I stopped and backtracked about ten paces in the direction we had just come from.

I motioned to him to stay where he was and indicated for him to make a cow call, and I moved off a few more paces and found a good shooting place beside a small poplar tree. The bull had heard the soft cow call that Eddie had made and let out a screaming bugle that goes right to your gut; it is the most exhilarating experience one can ever have.

The elk are like ghosts and can appear as quiet as a church mouse. I saw him after his bugle; he was about 75 yards off, and he was still trying to circle us, and I knew it would scent us soon. I had a decent shot, but he was still behind some scrubs, but as he moved, I found my shooting lane. When he had moved almost to this hole in the bushes, I made a little elk chirp, and he froze right where I wanted him. I whistled my 7mm right through his lungs, and he bolted, but I knew my shot was good.

I turned to look at Eddie, who gave me the thumbs up and indicated to hold tight. I knew this was the best thing to do, sit tight and listen, the bull had crashed off, but with a lung shot, they do not go far. We waited about ten minutes, and Eddie and Lars had moved over to me. Eddie was whispering that I know my shit and knew the bull was circling us. Lars was quiet, and I thought in shock, but smiling.

We tracked the bull as lung shots leave a lot of light colored blood, and Eddie said, "Lung shot". The bull was down and not moving as we approached. I poked him from behind and let out an Aboriginal yell that startled Eddie and scared Lars a lot. We shook hands, and Eddie got surprised as I put my hands on the elk's head and gave my thanks to spirits like I always do. I explained to Lars that I always thank Mother Earth for this gift, and I knew I had made a special friend in Eddie. He said, "Most hunters are not as considerate as you," and he respected that very much.

Lars was as shocked as a city boy from Stockholm, Sweden could be on his first day out elk hunting. His comments included a lot of OMG and other gibberish in Swedish that had me and Eddie laughing. Eddie was very thankful as I helped him skin and gut the elk. He commented that few hunters help with the skinning and gutting. It was noon, and we had our elk down.

Eddie had already been in contact with the camp, and a camp hand was on his way with two pack horses and would meet him partway. Eddie asked if I was ok staying with the elk, and he would hurry back with the two pack horses. Eddie advised staying alert as a big grizzly had been hanging out in this area.

Eddie left, and Lars and I sat near the elk, and Lars wished we had some rum to celebrate. I pulled a mini flask out of my pack and handed it to Lars, and he was laughing about my preparation. He talked a mile a minute and was sending Ingrid and Ina photos with his cell phone. I was not sure of cellular coverage where we were, but his texts were going through.

I knew Eddie would take more than an hour to return, and I was watchful and listening for any grizzly. The grizzly has adapted over the years so that when they hear a rifle shot near them, it can lead them to meat. About one hour had passed since the shot that took down the elk, and I was nervous because I had heard some movement in the bush near where we were sitting. We were on a log about thirty yards from the elk, and the sounds were beyond the elk.

Wild animals move about in the bush, as quietly as a field mouse, and I was using binoculars to watch the area where I had heard some noise. Lars was chattering away and had no clue what I was keeping watch for or what I was looking for. I whispered for him to be quiet, and I picked up my rifle. The grizzly appeared like a ghost about ten yards on the other side of the elk from us. The wind was swirling, and I knew he was likely getting some of our scent, but the elk smell was masking our smell, and maybe he was hungry, so a little less cautious.

"Elk Hunt"

Eddie and I had split the elk into four quarters. The grizzly cautiously approached the elk, and I was extremely nervous as he had not seen us, but I thought it was likely he was getting some of our scent. He grabbed one front quarter without the neck attached in his mouth and turned and walked away with it, with no effort at all. He was a monster, I thought, but had never been that close to a grizzly, but the way he picked up the 250-pound quarter of meat, I knew he was big.

I had determined to leave the grizzly take some meat, as I did not know if the outfitter had any grizzly tags. You cannot shoot any grizzlies without a tag. Lars was pushing against me, and I could feel him shaking. I whispered for him to stay where he was as I was going to determine if the grizzly was moving off. He was not happy with that prospect, and I assured him I was not going very far.

I could hear, and I tracked the grizzly about 100 yards, and as I approached him, I heard him crash off, so he must have heard and scented me and left with his meat. I caught a glimpse of him moving up a ridge about 100 yards away, and I had time to take out my cell phone and video him. He disappeared over the ridge, and I knew we were ok, so I returned to the elk. Lars was quite happy to see me and thought he may have wet himself only a little, he said, and was really embarrassed.

266

I was laughing at his expense, but knew his dilemma; I had been in that situation once when I was being hunted by a cougar. Eddie showed up about fifteen minutes later, and Lars was babbling away in a mixture of Swedish and English, all garbled, and I explained to Eddie about the grizzly visit, and I let him have a quarter.

I showed Eddie the video I had of the grizzly, and he said, That's him; he is a good one. Eddie was pissed, and after he looked at the paw imprints in the mud, he said, "Yup, that is the one that has bothered me twice now and maybe once too many."

We loaded the elk on the two pack horses, and again, Eddie was impressed that I knew a diamond hitch pattern to tie the elk onto the pack saddles. One horse had the two hind quarters to balance his load, and the other horse had the remaining front quarter, and Eddie had a small battery-powered Sawzal, which we used to cut the rack of horns out, and tied it along with the front quarter.

We arrived back in camp, and there was lots of cheering and back slapping, and all shared rum. Nick, Bob had not been successful, but had some bulls that were talking to them.

We had fresh elk tenderloin for supper, and Lars said he had never tasted anything so good. He had snuck off to our cabin and changed his pants and shorts, and I never mentioned this to anyone. Day one elk hunt was a blast, and I had the largest elk horns I had ever shot, and the outfitter, Jake, said that it was not a big one, but very respectable. The lively conversation around the dinner table and later in their lounge was centered on my elk kill and the grizzly taking a quarter.

Jake told me I had done the right thing and asked me if I wanted a grizzly; he had a spare tag. This pleased Eddie, who said, "Great, that bastard has taken his last piece of elk from me." Apparently, this had happened twice before, once taking the whole animal and caching it.

Sept 11, I told Eddie that the next day he can go with Trevor, the other guide, and Nick and Bob if he chooses. I would sleep in with Lars and practice shooting with him. Eddie chose to go scout the grizzly as he now knew he could guide me to take him.

I spent the morning with Lars shooting my rifle, and he caught on real quick. I said, "You are ready to take your first elk," "Shit, I have never shot a gun or killed anything," he said. Eddie arrived back and asked if I wanted to go scout the grizzly with him. Lars was yawning and still had jet lag, so he was only too happy to stay in camp and sleep.

Eddie and I set off to the same area of the elk kill. He explained that he had shot a deer and hung it in a tree near the elk kill; he was sure the grizzly would come and claim the deer. We got near the spot where he had killed the deer, and the horses were very nervous because of the grizzly smell. We backtracked a couple of hundred yards and tied up the horses.

We approached the deer kill spot, and the deer was gone, and Eddie tracked the grizzly to where he had buried the deer under some brush and logs. We left the area, and he told me we would give him a day to feed on the deer before we hunt him.

When we arrived back at camp later, Trevor, Bob, and Nick were back, having played with bull elk all day, but the elk won. Day 2, we had one elk and prospects for filling our tags and maybe a grizzly to boot.

That night, Bob was curious about how I was going to manage the costs, and Lars, who had multiple rums, said, "Shit, he is not paying anything, this hunt is on me, I have never seen or experienced anything like it, it is the least I can do." The rum was talking, but he could do it if he chose.

Day 3, Eddie, Lars, and I were on our way at 6 am. We arrived in a different area; we did not want to disturb the grizzly. There was a good sign, and the area was a little more open with few big trees and lots of small spruce. We had good elk sign, and Eddie had stopped on a ridge to cow call. He also tried a small satellite bull call, and when he did that, he got a bugle in response almost immediately.

"Elk Hunt"

That is usually the indication that a herd bull is warning the satellite bull that he is aware of him and to stay away. We backtracked a little, tied up the horses, and continued on foot. Lars was nervous as he was the shooter today.

When Eddie thought we had a good position for our possible sit, we took positions to wait for a bull to come and challenge. I was beside Lars and would coach him. Eddie gave a cow call again, and he got the same herd bull answering immediately. He continued with a lost cow call, and then after about five minutes, he gave the satellite bull call again. The herd bull was now screaming at us; he was pissed at this possible imposter.

I had cut a small sapling for Lars to use as a rest, as there were no trees around to use. The herd bull had to be less than 100 yards by the sound, and he made quite a racket by demolishing dry willows. He was angry and trying to get the imposter to leave.

Eddie did more lost cow calls, and the bull was trying to tell her to come to him. He showed himself about 75 yards away, and I whispered to Lars that now is the time, aim for the lung. He was shaking, and I helped him steady the gun. He aimed and squeezed slowly, and I knew the hit was good by the bull's reaction as he bolted. Eddie gave me the thumbs up, and we were quiet and waiting.

The bull made lots of noise, crashing through brush on his escape route. We gave him about ten minutes, and then Eddie tracked him. He left a good blood trail and was lying about another 75 yards from where he was shot. Lars was still shaking and laughing hysterically. He did ok for a complete greenhorn that shot for the first time in his life yesterday.

The bull was definitely a herd bull; his body was bigger than mine, and he had a seven-by-seven rack. Lars was blabbering away in Swedish, and I was trying to calm him down as he was over the hill, excited. We shook hands many times, and we took a lot of photos, and then the work started.

Lars had calmed down and was interested enough to help and hold legs. We skinned, gutted, and quartered him, and Eddie had called camp. He told them his location, and they were able to bring two quads to the location. Cell phone technology is great, as Eddie was able to PIN our location and send it to the guys in camp. They could enter the PIN identifier coordinate into the quad GPS and come right to our location. Lars was amazed.

We were back in camp before noon and hung Lars's elk on the meat pole. Lars was enjoying the backslapping and cheers from all, like he was a movie star.

After dark, Trevor, Nick, and Bob arrived in camp. They also had luck. They had come upon two herd bulls fighting, and that allowed them to sneak up within 100 yards, and they got both bulls.

The supper and the après supper talks were so much fun. Everyone had an elk, and it was only day 3. Lars was cheered for his first time elk kill, and actually, it was my son Nick's first elk kill also. Bob and I had bagged elk together before. The talk was then drifting to the possible grizzly hunt the next day.

Sept 14, everyone knew that I was the shooter for the grizzly hunt, but they all wanted to come. Eddie was not enthused as he said there must be absolute quiet and listen to all his instructions. We were up and departed at six am.

When we were a long way from the grizzly meat cache, Eddie stopped, and we all tied up our horses. A grizzly relies on its smell for recognizing danger, and Eddie had planned our approach so we were downwind from the cache. When we were still with the horses, Eddie had drawn a map on the ground and indicated where he would put the group of spectators and where he and I would approach from.

At about 150 yards from the cache, Eddie whispered to me that the cache was disturbed, but he could not see the grizzly. It was almost full light, and we moved one or two steps at a time. Eddie stopped, and I knew he was worried by his body language;

he turned to me and indicated that he smelled the grizzly, which meant that he was close and hunting us.

No sooner had Eddie given me the nose sign than, to our right, about 40 yards away, the bush exploded. The grizzly came out of the bush and was in a full charge at us. I had no time to think and fired just below his head for a full chest shot. This dropped him to the ground, and he was now giving me a broadside shot, and I had a second round into his neck just behind his head. He was crawling toward us with his front legs, and Eddie slammed him with two slugs from his 12-gauge. We never took our eyes off him for a full five minutes until Eddie gave me the thumbs up, and I was able to relax.

I was shaking pretty bad when the gang arrived, and Nick held me for a minute and said, "Good shooting, you old bastard." Eddie came over and hugged me and said, "You had him on his knees before I had turned, and then slammed another into his neck in seconds." He took my rifle, examining it, and wondered how I fired two shots so quickly. I said the fear of God and lots of practice. There was laughter and cheers all around, and I just sat on a log for a good half hour to stop the shaking. Eddie asked me if I checked my pants because he said, "I thought I may have shit mine."

"Elk Hunt"

Eddie completed the skinning, and I wanted a full head and claws on a flat rug. Lars was so over the hill amazed and was busy sending texts with photos and videos to Ina and Ingrid. Ina came on the phone with a video call and was scolding me profusely as she knew I would be up to no good and possibly harm to myself. I said, "I will try most things so long as they don't kill me, but I do not want to do this again."

Back at camp, Trevor and a camp hand had hauled Nick and Bob's elk to camp, and they were hanging on the meat pole. There were many photos taken with each of us with our elk, and then group shots as well. I could not have asked for any better a hunt, albeit the grizzly charge was a twist that is part of hunting, but not to be repeated in my future. The grizzly was an eight-foot monster, and Jake had measured its skull and thought he might make Boone and Crochet's record book.

We had a rambunctious evening with many rounds of rum, the stuff Lars brought, and the stuff the hunters that canceled had ordered. Day five, we were all packing, and the outfitters crew was very busy. They meat would fly out with us to be hung at a butchers, cut and wrapped, and sausage made.

It's amazing how much a Twin Otter airplane can carry. Four men and their gear, four elk, four racks, and a grizzly hide, and we lifted off without any issue and arrived in Fort Nelson safely. The

274

outfitter had the butcher meet the airplane and took all the meat, while the horns and grizzly hide would go with me in Bob's truck.

Lars came with me, Nick, and Bob, and we arrived at Nick's home on **Sept 15**. We all relaxed at Nick's after a fabulous hunt, and I told everyone that it was actually half price, as the four hunters who canceled forfeited their down payment, and it went towards our fee. I told them I had given all the staff there a tip of $500 each because of our break on the cost, except Eddie, who got $500 and my rifle as well. He said it was good luck and he will use it for his hunting gun after this.

Bob left the next morning, and I took Lars to Kelowna with me. Nick went back to work and was so thankful for the hunt; he did not know when he could ever find the time or money to do it himself. I had called ahead to see if Lars and I could spend the night at Chris's. Chris did not know where I had got to, but welcomed me. When we got there, Chris was surprised it was not just me, and he said, " Ike is full of surprises."

Lars arranged a flight out of Kelowna to Vancouver the next day, then on to Iceland and Sweden. He was talking with Chris nonstop, and that is unusual because Chris often carries the lion's share of the talking. They got along like old buddies, and Chris was reminiscing about the trip when he had joined Les on his world-traveling journey.

"Elk Hunt"

We got Lars on his flight the next day, and back at Chris's, we talked lots more about my plans with Ina, getting married, having a child, and I said, "It will all be in a book I am writing," and explained that to him and Brenda. They were very enthusiastic about this possible novel from a redneck like me.

Chapter 16

"A Cattle Ranch in Canada"

The next day, **Sept 17**, I met with the realtor and he took me to his office and we reviewed a number of small cattle ranches that he thought met my criteria. We went and looked at two, and they were not suitable.

The next day, Chris came with me and we traveled farther south near Penticton and looked at a ranch with 200 acres, good buildings for the cattle, and a gorgeous log home. It had about 10 acres of fruit trees, 100 acres of bottom land near the river for hay, and it was irrigated. The property backed onto a 500-acre grazing lease. It was in receivership and bids were being accepted till the first of October, when it was scheduled in court.

Chris had gone through this process with his current home and knew the ins and outs. He told us that sometimes there is shady business, and bids come in at the last minute and are just over the highest bid. The last-minute bidders sometimes have inside information.

"A Cattle Ranch in Canada"

The realtor wanted to stop for a meal in Penticton, and he was on his phone steadily. He seemed to be talking with contacts about the receivership details. He finally was off his phone and able to relate to me and Chris that properties like this are a money pit and that the bids already in are quite low.

Chris looked at me and winked. Chris asked the realtor how he knew this information and what the current highest bid was. He was not providing that information. But he said his gut feeling was that if a bid of about half a million came in, it might be sufficient. But he warned that it was in need of lots of work and money.

Chris and I left and discussed this on the way to his place. Chris said that it was indeed a money pit, but fixed up and with cattle running, the orchard maintained, and the hay land utilized, it could be worth four times that or more. Chris lived here and explained that the real estate market had peaked and was now on a downward slide, and the economy was not doing great.

That night, I was on a video call with Ina, and after all our conversation about the hunt and other things, I mentioned the ranch that Chris and I saw today. She said that it sounds like I should research further and maybe place a bid for it.

Chris and I met the realtor there the next day, and we had an in-depth look at all the buildings and land. We went for a short drive up into the grazing lease. We made notes about all its needs and potential problems that we could find. The realtor advised that he had further calls with some staff he knew at the courthouse, and once again suggested that his gut feeling was that one half million would likely be the highest bid.

We went back to Chris's place, and we discussed that the bidding process can be rigged with inside information. We thought we might have that inside information.

The next day, we went to the Penticton courthouse and put my bid of $500,000 with a 10 % deposit that must accompany the bid, $50,000. If your bid was not accepted or a higher bid was received, the deposit was returned. The bad part was that we now had 11 days to wait.

That night, I discussed with Ina, and she said she would rub my Buddha for good luck. She was complaining that my trip was longer than I had suggested, and she misses me. Chris and Brenda asked about the Buddha, and I explained.

I left on **Sept 21**, and drove back to Edmonton to look at houses with Kim and Colby. I met Kim, and she was still a little skeptical about me buying her a house. She had given it more thought and was unsure about where to live.

I met with Colby and my ex-wife, Diane, and asked if they had decided where Colby would like to have a house.

I spent the night at my friend Peter's place, and we caught up on all my travels and experiences. Peter and Margo were impressed that an old guy could pack so much into less than one year.

The next day, Colby called me and said he and his mother had talked to Ina and realized that I was not joking, and they had discussed him possibly buying Diane's home. She wanted to sell and then rent from him. It would be an ironic change, but would suit her needs as she could then be mortgage-free and decide on retiring early and move to her cottage that she had inherited in Nova Scotia. It was unusual circumstances, but it seemed to fit both of them. She commented that "At least she would pay rent," which brought a good laugh.

I said they should make the choices and let me know, and I could provide the money as soon as the papers are complete.

The next day, **Sept 21**, Colby called and he informed me that he and his mother had agreed to complete the deal, and her lawyer was completing the paperwork. I was now one down and two to go for plans for my children.

Colby had called Kim, and after much discussion, she was finally realizing I was not joking. She was uncertain about where to live; she wanted to go back to Vancouver Island, but she said there is little work there. She was leaning towards Edmonton and the area she is familiar with, and all her friends live near.

I went to meet her and we went for supper. I suggested that maybe she look outside of her comfort box and consider Valmont, and there is this one restaurant there that could open full-time if she is the full-time cook. She thought about that but needed time to decide.

I told her to take her time, and she thought I was some kind of lucky guy. I explained it was all because of a Buddha. She did not know what to think of that.

Sept 25, I drove to Valmont, and Nick and I had a good chat. He told me Kim had called and asked him if he knew all about my good fortune. He told her it was all true and then told her about our hunt and meeting my future father-in-law. She asked him about a restaurant in Valmont that I mentioned to her, and it needs a cook, and I suggested that she move there.

Nick was not pleased with this suggestion, as he and Kim don't get along either. But he did think it would be a good fit; he knew the owners and could go talk with them.

Nick and I worked out some details about him receiving just money from me, as he already has his home. It would work best for him, he could work a little less and spend more time on completing his shop-home and his plans to be off the grid, which takes money, lots of work, and time.

I spent another day with Nick. His friend Marty was now apprenticing with Nick as a plumber, and Nick could soon do all his business without his friend Tamara as part of it, doing the front-end stuff, but she also needed to be paid.

Sept 28, I left for Peachland and stayed with Chris and Brenda. I relaxed after my whirlwind hunt and trip to Alberta. Chris and I caught up on all my experiences, and he was really impressed with my possible novel. He read what I had written so far and said it interested him and wondered how it would end. I explained that it will include this trip to Canada, and then this story will end in Sweden.

I explained that maybe I will try for a second book about the rest of Les's trip through Africa and South America. He went with me to look at the ranch again, and we visited Bob in Penticton. He wanted to go with us to look at the ranch himself. Bob suggested that if I get the ranch, we could build a 2000 plant grow operation there, and the rent can go to someone he knows. It was an interesting business proposition that I likely could not discuss with Ina. Bob liked the location so much that he said if I could subdivide a few acres for him, he would build his own home there.

Oct 1 rolled around, and Chris and I were at the courthouse at opening time, which was the date bids closed for the ranch. We found the courtroom assigned for the judicial proceedings and took a seat. After the judge entered and things got underway, there were a number of other matters dealt with, and the ranch bids were opened. The clerk handed them to the judge one by one, and there were not many, maybe six.

I was nervous as hell, and when the judge had all the bids in front of him, he read them off from lowest to highest. When he got to mine, I thought it was the highest, but he then took another one and read the bid, $505,000, shit, I thought some bastard had brought in a bid just in time and knew what my bid was.

The judge was quiet and was in discussion with his court clerk. He then told the courtroom that the last bid did not have the ten percent deposit and, therefore, it did not meet the rules and was not acceptable. A man jumped up and asked to approach the bench. There was considerable discussion, and the judge just listened. The guy was getting upset and trying to explain that he needed more time, as he had only heard about it a few days ago and could not provide the deposit in the time frame.

The judge asked him to take a seat and told the courtroom there is no room for this kind of complaint, that this last-minute bid was only yesterday when it came in, and therefore it was disqualified.

The guy was yelling, and the judge asked him to be removed from the courtroom. He asked if Mr Gramlich or his lawyer were present, and I stood up. He asked me to approach the bench, where I was required to sign multiple documents which stipulated that within a time limit to either pay the balance or arrange financing.

He asked about my name; he seemed to be familiar with it. My brother stood up and asked to approach the bench. He told the judge that he recognized him, explaining that years ago, he had been the successful bidder for a house in Peachland. A similar last-minute bid had been made, but it was not accepted for the same reason. The judge was laughing and said he rarely forgets a face, and now he remembers Chris. He said, "Good luck to you," and **I had a ranch**.

When we left the courthouse, we were approaching my SUV, and the guy from the courthouse who was upset came running up to us. He was complaining and almost crying; he was putting on a great act. Chris told him to get lost, and I thought we may have a difficult situation on our hands. The guy told Chris that if he were not so damn big, he would kick the shit out of him. I stepped around Chris and said, "I am not so damn big, and that is my ranch."

The guy was sizing me up, and when he turned to go away, I knew he was going to turn back and throw a haymaker at me. That is exactly what happened; he whirled around and took a wild swing at me. I was ready for it, ducked under his swing, and kneed him in the groin. As his head came down, I hit him with an uppercut and he went down like a sack of spuds.

Chris told him to stay down, or my little brother will do you some serious damage. We got in my SUV, and Chris said, "Ike, you still have it." We called my friend Bob, who lives in Penticton, and went over for a couple of drinks to celebrate and told him about the unsuccessful bidder.

Bob was relating a similar incident outside a Yellowknife bar, where he said Ike was acting really scared with this big mouth, and when the guy was not expecting it, he had a boot in the groin and about ten punches till he was flat on his ass and bleeding like crazy.

Bob was really interested in discussing more about the ranch and a future grow-op there.

Chris and I went back to his home and relaxed. I sent Ina a text about the results of the ranch bid. She called me right back and was so excited; she wanted to fly out and look at it herself. I told her we have all our lives to spend there, and it needs a lot of work.

She needs her rest, and another whirlwind tour would not do her and our baby any good.

I explained my plans for my son in Spruce Grove to buy his mother's home, and the possible plans for Kim and Nick. She was happy I was settling all my planned tasks for this trip. She told me that Lars is a very popular man at his club, where he shows videos and tells the story of the hunt about a hundred times.

She said there are a couple of club members who want to come for a hunt someday. I told her I still had to arrange for shipment of the meat to Sweden, and he could arrange a big elk meat feast at the club.

She was looking forward to my return, which I said would be about one to two weeks. She told me to stay out of trouble or danger, but I had not told her about the guy at the courthouse.

Chris and I sat down and made a list of tasks to do at the ranch. I would contact multiple contractors to complete much of the work, and when I am not here, Chris could help to manage these contractors. He was enthused with this project as he has time and has lots of experience with this type of work and with managing contractors.

We went to the ranch and have now completed a more in-depth research of all the required tasks that needed attention. We spent hours checking every nook and cranny for difficulties that often don't become apparent at first glance.

The house was in great shape, but we made a list which included having all the utilities checked out, for the main house and all the outbuildings as well. Chris had two contractors in mind, one for all the electrical and one for plumbing, heating, and sewer. I told him Nick would be my choice for plumbing, heating, and sewer, but he is too far away and busy.

The main yard fencing needed repairs, and likely lots of the other property fencing. I wasn't entirely sure about the requirements for fencing on the grazing lease. There were two main barns, one a large loafing shed and the other a main floor with a dozen horse stalls and a second floor open loft for feed. They were in top shape, just needing some TLC and paint on the barn.

The grounds all around the yard were in need of work of mowing the grass, trim hedges, and perform other landscaping tasks. The orchard needed a horticulturist to come and complete a review of all the fruit trees condition and the necessary work on the entire 10 acres for drainage and weeds, etc.

I would need the orchard and 80-acre hay field irrigation system checked out including condition of the equipment.

Our list was large and a very daunting task with so many different areas and specialty contractors required. I was a little worried about this, as I would have to be here for most of it, as Chris has his own life and could only help so much.

As we drove around the outside property boundaries, we noticed something that we had missed. There was a creek flowing through the northeast corner of the property. We got out looking this over, and I was very excited because there were elk dung pellets all over and many sleeping beds. The elk like running water to drink, and I was assuming they were coming down from the mountain with the 500-acre grazing lease. Wow, what a bonus, maybe my own herd of wild elk used this property for their winter grazing and watering.

This added bonus had me extremely happy with the purchase, even though it was a large task to complete all the work. We completed our inspection and work lists and stopped by Bob's place in Penticton.

Bob was looking forward to helping when he could and was as excited as I was when he heard about the elk. He warned that poaching would be tricky, as most of the herd would likely have GPS implants for the wildlife officers and environmentalists to utilize for management and protection of the herd.

On **Oct 10**, I was busy calling multiple contractors, meeting with them to arrange an inspection, and getting quotes. Over the next week, I had many of them hired, and much of the work would progress in the next few months.

I changed the locks on many buildings and installed an alarm system, which included 24-hour video monitoring cameras in multiple locations. The company monitored this from their main office and could react to any suspicious activity with its mobile crew or alert the police.

There were still lots more contractors to research and hire, but what needed to be addressed to bring the property to a safe and livable environment were in progress. I took lots of videos and sent these on to Ina, and daily we discussed my progress. She was amazed that I knew all this stuff and was accomplishing so much.

She was very busy at work, and the videos I watched showed her getting bigger with the progressing pregnancy. Her Doctor suggested all systems were a go and she was doing great. I could not wait to get back and rub her tummy and my Buddha.

All the legal paperwork from the courts and land titles had come through to my lawyer, and I arranged for the balance of the property payment to be completed. I could not have been a happier man, so much had happened since I left Vancouver on Monday,

"A Cattle Ranch in Canada"

Jan 10, 2027, nine months ago. How could this be? Was it all too good to be true??

I had been in contact with Kim, and she was thinking of moving to Valmont. Nick had spoken with the restaurant owner, and he was interested in meeting Kim and discussing a full-time job there as the manager and the head chef combined position. She was apprehensive about this, with changing her life this drastically, but was going to travel out to meet the owner.

I arranged to meet her there in two days and drove to Valmont on **Oct 17**. Kim came with her friend Chrissie, who had management experience with a number of restaurants in Edmonton and had her own car. Kim had a driver's license but used public transportation or rode her bicycle.

I met Kim, Chrissie, and the restaurant owner, Jerry, at the Dasol Restaurant. We toured the dining area and kitchen. Chrissie and Kim looked at everything and were not impressed with the equipment and its condition. The owner explained that, with not being open much and a lack of staff, he was often left holding the bag and had to do much of the cleaning and maintenance work, and did not want to spend money, as income was not good.

It was a catch-22 situation for him, and he was at odds with keeping it open or hiring someone like Kim. He explained that if he saw potential for keeping it open more, he could justify

290

spending money on some equipment improvements. They talked for a couple of hours, and Kim and Chrissie wanted to talk about the difficulties and possibilities.

Chrissie was very experienced at this game and advised that the place needed some serious equipment improvements and a complete cleaning and sanitizing. She did speculate that it could be a big challenge, but had good potential; the layout was good, the dining area was pleasant, the kitchen needed work, and the location was good. She actually considered moving herself as she advised that the full-time management and full-time cook were two jobs, not one.

We went together and looked at four different homes with a realtor I had contacted. The prices surprised me; Chrissie and Kim, as Edmonton prices are much higher. They were impressed with one home that was ready to move into and was listed at $225 thousand.

I was putting together numbers based on Colby's house purchase of $425 thousand. I threw a carrot out, proposing that maybe a home like this in this price range could leave $200 thousand for a down payment on the restaurant. This was a completely different proposal from just buying Kim a home. Kim was thinking of my proposal because she had discussed it with Colby about buying Diane's house.

Kim and Chrissie were quiet, trying to digest all this information and the possibilities. It would need much more study, including whether the owner was willing to sell and the price, and whether the girls would take this opportunity.

We left it in that status, and they had to return to Edmonton.

I called the restaurant owner and met him at the restaurant. I asked him what he thought about the girls and their assessment of his business. He thought they knew what they were talking about, but was not sure what to do; he thought he would just like to sell the damn place, was the way he put it. I asked him how much it was worth.

He was quiet, realizing I was maybe their backer and then asked me my interest. I told him my interest was in an opportunity for my daughter, but the girls had no money. He was not sure, but thought the building and land were likely worth about $350 thousand, and the way things were in his life and the status of the business not doing much, he was willing to look at offers.

I told him I would think about it and contact the girls, as they were both thinking of moving out of Edmonton. He said he used to be busy, but then trying to find staff to keep it open more was a nightmare.

That night, I called Kim and talked over the possibilities of them buying the place, as I had gone to see the owner to talk turkey. She told me that I do not fuck around, and it interested her and she would call Chrissie. We had a video call an hour later, and the girls were willing to maybe give it a shot.

I went to talk it over with Nick, and he was surprised that they came out, especially Chrissie, as she had a good management job with Moxies. I told him of the owner's thoughts to just get rid of the place. I told him of Kim and Chrissie's interest in possibly buying the place, and he was thinking that with the two of them, they may have a chance to make a go of it.

I met the owner the next morning at the restaurant, and I said I wanted to talk about purchasing his business. He asked if I was thinking of an offer. I explained that the business position was not in good shape, and I had not even looked at his books. He was reluctant to open his books for viewing, sometimes that can open a can of worms with the tax man??

I thought about it and wondered how low I should consider, and then told him I could consider an offer of $250 thousand. He did not just reject the offer, so I knew he might be willing to take his losses and be done with it. He wanted time to consider, and I knew I had him by the balls, so to speak.

"A Cattle Ranch in Canada"

After meeting him, I went back to Nick's place and called Kim and Chrissie with the update. They were excited but apprehensive about all the difficulties involved. I left to drive back to Chris's place in Peachland and hoped I had a path forward for Kim.

That night, I discussed with Chris my plans for Kim, Nick, and Colby. He was impressed that I was giving them all a chance to get ahead. I told him it would cost me about 1.5 million and would be money well spent.

I called Ina that night, and she was wondering how I found all the time to do these things. She agreed that the money I was thinking of for my children was still half a million less than what we planned.

On **Oct 20,** I received a call from Jerry, the restaurant owner, who requested more money. However, I wasn't surprised when I presented the final offer, as I had mentioned when we first met. He was willing to take the offer. Wow, again so many Wow's in my life, and bottom line "Talk is cheap, but money buys whiskey."

I called Kim with the news, and she was ecstatic but worried. She said they had talked about the restaurant, and with a good cleaning and sanitizing; it could manage the way it was. They could improve as the need arose and their cash flow was positive. She told me thank you so much, she would have never believed this was possible.

I had settled with Colby and Kim, and Nick just needed cash, so that was settled also. Now I just needed to look after the money pit, my ranch.

Over the next week, I met with many contractors, some with bids and proposals. The electrical contractor had a list of required upgrades and maintenance items he could complete in the next month. The plumber, heating, and sewer had good news, he had completed some maintenance on this property, so he knew the condition of most everything and his work could be completed in the next week.

I had met a fencing contractor, who was a property owner nearby and knew this property well, and could complete all the fencing on the 200 acres in a month, but the grazing lease would have to be inspected, and then he could give me a better idea.

A friend of Chris's had inspected the house with Chris, and we met to discuss some improvements to the house and buildings. He had a list we went through, and I agreed with most of his proposals, axed some, and told him kitchen improvements would have to wait for the woman.

A big-ticket item was replacing about half the house windows. He would take about 3-4 months, depending on the supply of the windows and his available time to dedicate to this project. He proposed to use my place as a fill-in for other larger projects he had in progress, and it would save me money doing it this way. I knew he would not screw me over since he was a good friend of Chris.

I had met a contractor who employed an orchard expert and would come up with plans for improvements and winter pruning. He would also inspect and develop an irrigation plan, as he knew an irrigation contractor.

Most of the tasks on Chris's and my lists were either in progress or would be soon. I met with Bob for some R&R at his place in the hot tub and pool. I had been running my feet off and needed to sit back and smell the roses, then figure out what was left to do.

I was considering a date for returning to Sweden, as I knew Ina was likely getting worried I would never finish my tasks here. We had originally thought I would be in Canada for about one month, and two months was fast approaching.

I thought I needed about another week to finalize all the odds and ends and hire the rest of the contractors, and I booked flights to **Sweden for Oct 28.**

Over the next week, many things were finalized. That included a trip to Valmont for the purchase of the Valmont restaurant for Kim. She had worked out a partnership with Chrissie that would see her still having the majority shares, and Chrissie's input would be on capital expenditures for the restaurant. This partnership and all arrangements for the business were their problem. Kim would own her house, the one we had looked at, and they would live together, and Chrissie would pay her rent.

Some of the ranch work was completed, some was in progress, and some things still needed to be finalized, but plans were in place. Chris was my contact here to meet with various contractors as required. I was set to go and really ready for some time away from this whirlwind of two months.

The elk meat was ready for shipment, and arrangements were to be made from Fort Nelson to wherever. I got together with Bob in Penticton and discussed the elk meat details. His meat would come directly here to his place, and Nick's meat would go to his place, and my meat would come with Bob's to his place. I bought a deep freeze, and Bob would receive it all at his home and put it in my freezer at the ranch.

We decided to have Lars's meat come with Bob's and my meat, and I would make necessary shipping arrangements for the required refrigerated shipment to Sweden.

Bob had delivered all the sets of horns and my grizzly hide to a taxidermist, and the mounting of the horns, the head and the feet of the grizzly were in progress.

"A Cattle Ranch in Canada"

Ina was so pleased to hear about all the arrangements, all the purchases, and we were still under budget from our limits set. She thought I managed my money with care and diligence. I was always impressed that she called it my money, not our money.

I arrived back in Stockholm, and Ina jumped into my arms at the airport. She was full of questions, and we could not wait to get to our house. We had a quick trip to the bedroom for a prayer session.

Chapter 17
"Life in Sweden"

Settling into a home life with Ina after the whirlwind trip to Canada was very relaxing and comforting. I had accomplished most of what I had planned on the trip, and as a bonus, I had the elk hunt with my son, my good buddy, and my future father-in-law.

Ina wanted more details on the hunt and was totally amazed at the size and strength of the grizzly. She asked what would have happened if you had not killed him. I said, "Maybe Eddie would have been able to stop him, but his back was to him, and the grizzly may have got him as he was turning around to shoot." I told her that neither of us may have made it.

She was not impressed with that assessment of the dire possibilities, but I said that is the chance you take when hunting, especially in the grizzly's home. What annoys them is when you infringe on their territory or come near their cache of meat. You are a threat they will try to eliminate.

"Life in Sweden"

We were invited over to Lars and Ingrid's for supper the next day. Lars was talking a mile a minute about the hunt, and I told him the meat is on its way. He still cannot believe what he had experienced and said, "If it was not for Ike, I would have never got an elk; he had to hold my gun steady." I told them it is called 'greenhorn jitters' or 'buck fever'.

I explained that hunting is learning to respect that you are in the wild animal's territory, and they usually have the upper hand. They rely on hearing and smell for their safety. I explained that the technique of attracting the animal by calling to them has everything to do with reproduction.

During the mating season, both males and females have attraction instincts and methods that help to ensure the females get bred and pregnant. The males are extremely excited and will make mistakes because of the extreme testosterone levels that cause irrational behavior, which will put them in danger. They become what we call "stupid", just like humans, which brought quite a laugh from all.

I suggested that I could talk for hours about the hunts I have had, some with circumstances similar to the grizzly bear hunt. Ingrid suggested that I write another novel after I finished the rest of my brother's world journey novels. She said, "Ike's 100 hunts and he is still alive." We all laughed at that.

Lars was anxious to get the elk meat and arrange a Canadian wild elk feast at his club. He told me that he had shown all the still shots, and especially the video of the grizzly bear charge and kill.

Lars had a very good camera on the trip and was quite an experienced photographer, so I knew that some of his photos and the video would be of excellent quality. I had not seen any of his shots or videos and was looking forward to them.

He said the gang at his club can't wait to have me narrate the grizzly charge. I said, "So I tell them how scared I was and I shit my pants." Everyone was laughing, and Ina said, "You did not fill your pants, did you?" I said, "No, but I sat down for thirty minutes till the shaking stopped." I admit that in my entire hunting experience, I had never been that close to a grizzly, never shot one, and do not want to shoot another one.

Lars commented that he was impressed with my gesture to mother earth, which included putting my hands on the animal and praying. I told them that I was just thanking my Buddha. Ingrid asked if I actually thank mother earth, and I admitted I did, it was an old habit from many years ago when a cougar hunted me. They all wanted this story.

I told them I was elk hunting and was tired, and I sat with my back to a big stump from a deadfall. I was elk cow calling and had lots of elk scent on my clothes. There were no answers to my calling, so I was so comfortable, and the sun was warming me nicely, and I fell asleep.

My spider instincts and maybe the smell of the cougar woke me, and a cougar was about 10 feet away and ready to spring. I had not moved and only opened my eyes. He sprang at me, and I rolled to my right side, and he caught my left leg with his paw and ripped through my pants and tore my leg open.

They were mesmerized, and Ingrid said, "I think this is one of your stories that is bullshit." I said "No" and I stood up, dropped my pants, and showed the 6-inch scar on the inside of my left leg. I said I was lucky I had not moved, and when I did, he was startled, with me rolling and only pawing me with a glancing blow. He bolted, and I managed a quick shot, and it killed him. After that experience, I started thanking mother earth for each gift.

Ina commented that she had seen the scar but never asked where it came from, and "Pull your damn pants up, please, Ingrid will get excited." Ingrid threw a pillow at Ina.

The way Ina, Ingrid, Lars, and I often joked and mostly had open conversations about everything was comforting and built a good relationship. The short time we had known each other and the unusual experiences we had together were helping build strong family bonding and a good atmosphere.

That night in bed, Ina and I were relaxed and reminiscing about our trip. We both were amazed at how short the time was since we met, and how outrageous and unusual our experiences were, and the positive outcome of almost everything. It was **Nov 15, 2025.** We were discussing Ina's pregnancy and both wished our child would be healthy and normal, boy or girl, it did not matter.

We wanted to live our lives to its fullest and were looking forward to completing the ranch plans and possibly living there, at least part-time.

I wanted to complete the rest of my brother's incredible world journey, although when was a big question, to what extent would I complete different sections, and how Ina and a child would fit into those plans.

Chapter 18

"Future Dreams and Plans for Ike and Ina"

How would my life as a potential writer pan out, or was I just a flash in the pan?

We wondered how a Lindgren and Gramlich family gathering would take place and when.

When would Ina and Ike get married?

How would Ike and Ina's offspring come into the world and grow up?

Would Ike and Ina have any other children with more extraction of sperm from Ike's nuts?

How long would Ike's virility last?

How long would Ike's health last till he started to put the wheels down?

Would the love between Ike and Ina be forever?

When Ike slowed down, would Ina look at other males or consider straying?

Would Ike and Lars and maybe some Swedish friends of Lars's go hunting in Canada?

Would Ike and Lars and maybe some Swedish friends of Lars's go hunting in Sweden or Finland?

Would Ike and Lars and maybe some Swedish friends of Lars's go ocean fishing in Sweden?

Would Ike and Lars and maybe some Swedish friends of Lars's go ocean fishing in Canada?

Are Garret and Anong managing better with the changes?

Are Colby and Kim settling into their new roles as homeowners?

Are Kim and Chrissie progressing to have a prosperous business?

So many possibilities to answer all the questions of this continuing life saga of **Ike and Ina**!!!!

www.ingramcontent.com/pod-product-compliance
Lightning Source LLC
Chambersburg PA
CBHW071711120626
46550CB00001B/182